Recipes from

WHAT'S COOKING

with
RUTH FREMES
Book Three

Recipes from

WHAT'S COOKING

with

RUTH FREMES
Book Three

🔷 METHUEN

Toronto   New York   London   Sydney   Auckland

Canadian Cataloguing in Publication Data

Fremes, Ruth, 1930–
    Recipes from What's cooking with Ruth Fremes

Collection of recipes from author's television
program, What's cooking with Ruth Fremes.
Includes index.
ISBN 0-458-95780-1 (v. 3).

1. Cookery.   I. What's cooking with Ruth Fremes
(Television program)   I. Title.

TX715.F73   641.5   C80-094824-6

Printed and bound in Canada
1 2 3 4 5   82   87 86 85 84 83

CONTENTS

Introduction 1
What Metric Changeover Means 3
Microwave Notes 7

1 / Hors d'Oeuvres and Appetizers 9

2 / Soups 17

3 / Beef, Pork, Veal and Lamb 25

4 / Poultry 47

5 / Fish 62

6 / Luncheon and Supper Main Dishes 74

7 / Vegetables 88

8 / Salads and Dressings 96

9 / Breads 103

10 / Muffins, Cakes and Cookies 110

11 / Desserts 122

12 / Et Cetera 144

Recipe Credits 151
Index 152

INTRODUCTION

It's the beginning of summer now as I put the finishing touches on the manuscript that will become Volume 3 in the series based on the television show *What's Cooking with Ruth Fremes*. Most of these recipes will not be aired until next fall or winter; some are favorites that were not ready for Volume 2 and are included here. I sincerely hope this book will be interesting, exciting and well used in your kitchen for years to come.

So much has happened this year! I have travelled to Europe and the Far East, to the United States and all across this great Canada of ours. Everywhere I travelled there were wonderful people eager to share their ideas and explain the traditions that help create their native cuisine. Among these were Theresa de Jesus in Bangkok, whose daughter Chiap gave birth to a son during my stay there, but who, nevertheless, spent hours chauffeuring me to the homes of friends so that I could learn and appreciate their Thai foods. Julia Child encouraged and taught me so much (she uses instant potatoes for her gnocchi, for instance) and her tireless assistant Rosemary Manell suggested using a potter's kiln baking tile in the oven to help make crusty pizza.

Mary Risley in San Francisco worked along with me to create a foolproof recipe for croissants while Toronto's Meta McCall added two touches (cake yeast and cold ingredients) that made them perfect.

We had exciting guests in Studio 7 this season. Few will forget Michael Vaughan's visit with his sea urchins and mussels; Harvey Kirck cooking barbecue sauce in spite of his diet; the taste of Bonnie Stern's cheesecakes and the inventiveness of Lucy Waverman's Chinese adaptations of classic French cuisine. Monda Rosenberg came with Christmas suggestions, the prettiest of which was a hot pasta tossed with chopped green onions and red caviar, topped with lots of grated Parmesan cheese.

I am fortunate to have the same loyal and faithful crew. Standing ever-ready with a missing spoon or whisk are those talented home economists, Barb Holland and Gerry Anthony who test, re-test and help to prepare the many recipes that find their way to your television screens and this book. Thanks to Barb we have been able to include Microwave instructions this season. And thanks to so many of you who have taken time from busy days to send notes of encouragement or suggestions for recipes. I read them all and use the ideas in designing the shows.

Just one final word of thanks must go to my editor, Ros Steiner. This will be the third book for Ros and me and I cannot imagine sharing my mistakes nor having my verbosity corrected by anyone else. How she manages to be firm yet charming remains a mystery. It is enough that she is available to me when I need her, positive, friendly and always helpful. I dedicate this book to her, to my viewers and to my granddaughters Shawna and Jenny, who made it on television this season for the first time!

Fondest wishes and bon appetit!

R.F.
June, 1982

What Metric Changeover Means

Ask anyone. Metric changeover means madness. Metric changeover means new beginnings in the kitchen. Metric changeover means that anyone who cooks must learn to do it all over again. Or does it?

Doesn't it simply mean a different terminology for the same old thing? Well, yes, it does. This book is not completely metric, but I have included conversion amounts for items such as meats, produce and packaged products that are sold by metric weight. The recipes here all were tested using the imperial system of measure; however, the metric equivalents provided will produce a similar result. The system that has been agreed upon by recipe writers is to give a range of amounts—such as "about 500 g"—and this signifies that a little more or a little less will not affect the finished dish significantly.

Next year I intend to use new metric recipes that I have gathered in my travels. It isn't advisable really to convert recipes. So, for the recipes I have here, use your regular imperial measures.

For new metric recipes, use the correct metric calibrations. These are not exactly the same as the imperial amounts, but they are similar. For instance, a metric measure of volume replaces an imperial one; likewise with weight. See the chart below.

Measurement language

Metric System	Imperial System
millilitre (mL)	fluid ounce
litre (L)	quart
gram (g)	ounce
kilogram (kg)	pound
degrees Celsius (°C)	degrees Fahrenheit
centimetre (cm)	inch

Here are some examples of common metric amounts.

250 mL	replaces an 8-ounce cup
15 mL	replaces 1 tablespoon
5 mL	replaces 1 teaspoon
5 cm	is about 2 inches
1 kg	is a little more than 2 pounds
500 g	is a little more than 1 pound
100°C	water boils
160°C	oven temperature for roasting

It won't cost much to start metric cooking—all that's needed are these few metric measuring utensils. You must have these though, because, as I said, although the measures appear to be similar, they are replacement sizes, not exact equivalents.

Liquid measures

Measurements of liquids should be read at eye level. The 250 mL line is a little below the rim so that the liquid will not spill over. The 250 mL measure is graduated in 25 mL divisions. For larger amounts of liquid there is a 500 mL and a 1 000 mL measure, graduated in 50 mL.

Four of these (4 x 250 mL) are equal to 1 litre. One litre is slightly less than 1 quart.

Dry measures

The set consists of three measures each designed to have given capacity when level full. The dry measure set includes a 50 mL, 125 mL, and a 250 mL measure.

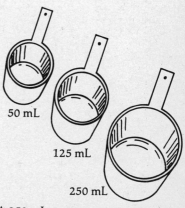

50 mL

125 mL

250 mL

A 250 mL measure compares to 1 "generous" cup.

Small Liquid and Dry Measures

The set includes five measures: 1 mL, 2 mL, 5 mL, 15 mL and a 25 mL (a typical coffee measure).

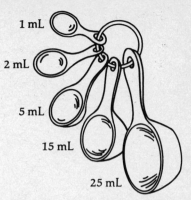

A 15 mL measure compares to 1 tablespoon.

Cooking Temperature

Metric recipes will express temperature in °C instead of Fahrenheit.

When using equipment with temperature dials or thermometers in degrees Fahrenheit, use this temperature conversion chart.

Replacements for Common Oven Temperatures

Celsius		Fahrenheit
60°C	—	140°F
70°C	—	150°F
80°C	—	170°F
100°C	—	200°F
120°C	—	250°F
140°C	—	275°F
150°C	—	300°F
160°C	—	325°F
180°C	—	350°F
190°C	—	375°F
200°C	—	400°F
220°C	—	425°F
230°C	—	450°F
240°F	—	475°F
260°C	—	500°F
270°F	—	525°F
290°C	—	550°F

The most commonly used temperatures have been boxed.

Cookware/Bakeware

Cookware and bakeware will be measured by volume just as the old cooking measures are. Small utensils will be measured in millilitres and larger pots and pans (1 000 mL or more) in litres. Besides the capacity, the label will also tell you what the utensil is to be used for —its generic name. You will see labels that read "Saucepan — 500 mL" or "Cake Pan — 2 L". No more trying to calculate or remember how many fluid ounces or cups in a quart or, worse still, how many fluid ounces or cups in an 8-inch pan.

The sizes of utensils are not changing much from their present sizes so that you can continue to use your existing pots and pans with metric recipes. When you want to find out their sizes, metrically speaking, just use one of your metric liquid measures to fill your pot or pan with water. This will tell you how many millilitres or litres your utensils hold. For those who need detailed information on cookware and bakeware, the Cookware and Bakeware Sector prepared *A Metric Guide for Cookware and Bakeware* which was published by the Canadian Home Economics Association. Single copies are available at $2.00 apiece from:

Canadian Home Economics
  Association
151 Slater Street
Ottawa, Ontario K1P 5H3

Ten copies may be purchased at a price of $15. Payment should accompany all orders.

COVERED SKILLET

FRY PAN

Base dimensions of 15 cm, 20 cm, 23 cm, or 25 cm, are the recommended sizes.

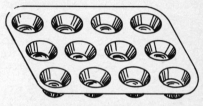

MUFFIN TIN or TART PAN

The recommended sizes for tart pans and muffin pans are 25 mL, 50 mL, 75 mL and larger sizes in multiples of 25 mL.

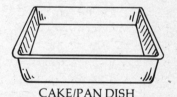

CAKE/PAN DISH

The recommended sizes for cake pans are 2 L, 2.5 L, 3 L, 3.5 L, 4 L and 5 L.

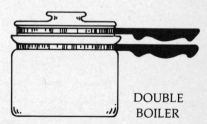

DOUBLE BOILER

The preferred sizes for double boiler vessels are 1.5 L, 2 L and 3 L.

For further information contact:

Metric Commission Canada
Box 4000
Ottawa, Ontario
K1S 5G8

Agriculture Canada
Sir John Carling Building
Ottawa, Ontario
K1A 0C7

MICROWAVE NOTES

We have included microwave instructions along with any recipes that can be adapted for microwave cooking. Aside from cooking or baking casseroles and cakes, though, a microwave should be used as a kitchen tool—something that makes ordinary cooking chores simpler. If you have a microwave oven, you may like to try some of these shortcuts.

- Before baking, use your microwave to plump raisins or currants. For each cup of dried fruit, add 1 teaspoon of water, juice or brandy. Stir with the raisins or currants. Then heat, uncovered, on full power for 15 seconds.
- To toast nuts or coconut, spread evenly over a microwave-safe plate. Loosely cover with paper toweling. Every half cup will take 2–3 minutes on full power. It's best not to do more than one cup at a time.
- To caramelize sugar, use a microwave-safe container—a 2-cup Pyrex measuring cup is a good choice. Measure ⅔ cup of granulated sugar and place in the container. Sprinkle with 2 tablespoons of water. Stir together with a fork just until blended. Heat for 4–4½ minutes on full power, until sugar turns a light amber color. Do not stir during the cooking time and be sure to use pot holders when you remove the dish from the microwave.
- When using unflavored gelatin, sprinkle the gelatin over the liquid as specified in the recipe or according to the directions on the package of gelatin. Make sure the gelatin-liquid mixture is in a small microwave-safe container. To dissolve the gelatin, heat the mixture in the microwave on full power for 20–45 seconds, until all granules seem to have dissolved.

- Pan-fried potatoes can be speeded up by precooking in the microwave. Thin-skinned potatoes are best. Scrub the skins. Dry thoroughly, then pierce the skin in several places. Cook on full power for half the time needed to bake the potatoes completely—i.e., 4 minutes for 2 potatoes, 8 minutes for 3 potatoes. Then immediately plunge into cold water to stop the cooking. Slice or chop and pan-fry just until golden brown.
- You can chop parsley more easily by slightly wilting several sprigs in the microwave before chopping.
- Clarifying butter is an easy procedure in the microwave. One cup of butter will need about 3 minutes on low or 30-percent power. Don't let it bubble. Skim off and discard the foam from the top of the clear clarified butter.
- To get the last few drops from a bottle of ketchup, remove the cap and heat for about 10 seconds.
- For easy juicing of oranges, lemons or limes, heat the fruit on full power for 15–20 seconds.

Softening

- To soften honey that has crystallized, remove the metal cap from the jar. Heat, uncovered, on full power for about 15 seconds for each cup of honey.
- A half cup of butter or margarine will soften in 10–15 seconds on full power. Be sure to remove any foil wrappings.
- Make bacon-slice separation easier by heating a pound of cold bacon for about 20 seconds on full power. Remember to remove any foil wrapping before heating.
- Soften cream cheese for easier spreading. Simply remove the foil wrapper and heat for 30–45 seconds on full power for a 125-gram package.
- If ice cream is too hard for scooping, place a one-litre container in the microwave and heat on full power for 15–30 seconds, depending on how solidly frozen the ice cream is.

HORS D'OEUVRES AND APPETIZERS

Snappy Cheese Apple 10

Cheese Wafers 11

Cheese Finger Snaps 10

Melon Wedges with Parma Ham 11

Late Day Pâté 14

John Clancy's Pâté en Croûte 12

Marinated Grouper 15

Escargots Bourguignon 16

Snappy Cheese Apple

An attractive centrepiece for a cheese tray.

Ingredients

3 cups shredded sharp Cheddar cheese (about 350 g piece)	2 tablespoons prepared mustard
1 cup shredded Swiss cheese (about 125 g piece)	1 teaspoon Worcestershire sauce
	$\frac{1}{8}$ teaspoon garlic powder
1 small package (125 g) cream cheese, softened	Chili powder
	Cinnamon stick
	Bay leaves

Method

Combine Cheddar cheese, Swiss cheese, cream cheese, mustard, Worcestershire sauce and garlic powder. Form into the shape of an apple and sprinkle generously with chili powder. Insert small piece of cinnamon and 1 or 2 bay leaves in top to resemble stem and leaves. Chill.

Cheese Finger Snaps

(Makes about 48 fingers)

Ingredients

1½ cups shredded medium or aged Gouda or Cheddar cheese	Pinch of cayenne
1 cup melted butter	1⅔ cups corn flakes cereal
1½ cups all-purpose flour	

Method

Combine cheese and butter in a bowl and mix with a fork until well blended. Combine flour and cayenne. Add to cheese mixture, then add corn flakes; mix to form a stiff dough. Roll out to ⅜ inch thickness. With a sharp knife, cut out fingers ½ inch wide and 2 inches long. Place them on ungreased baking sheets, leaving space between the fingers. Bake in a 325°F oven for 20–25 minutes until very lightly browned. Cool. Store in an airtight container in a cool place.

Cheese Wafers

These simple nibblers may be stored in a cookie tin for a week or wrapped tightly in the freezer for three months. (Makes 36 wafers)

Ingredients

2 cups sharp Cheddar or Gouda cheese, grated	2 cups all-purpose flour
2 cups rice crispies cereal	¼ teaspoon salt
1 cup butter or margarine	¼ teaspoon garlic powder
	Dash red pepper

Method

Preheat oven to 350°F. Mix ingredients well, roll into balls and press with a fork. Place on an ungreased cookie sheet and bake for 20 minutes or until lightly browned.

Melon Wedges with Parma Ham

This first-course dish introduces any dinner party with flair. It can be prepared ahead of time and arranged on the plate without any last-minute fuss. Serve with Pepper Mayonnaise (below). (Serves 4)

Ingredients

1 small, ripe canteloupe	4 lettuce leaves
4 thin slices Parma ham	

Method

Remove skin and seeds from the canteloupe and cut into 4 wedges. Roll Parma ham slice loosely around each wedge and place on lettuce leaf.

Pepper Mayonnaise

Ingredients

1 teaspoon green peppercorns	1 teaspoon lemon juice
⅓ cup mayonnaise	Salt

Method

Mash half the peppercorns with a fork. Add mayonnaise, lemon juice and salt to taste, then sprinkle with remaining peppercorns. Serve with ham and melon.

John Clancy's Pâté en Croûte

Pâté en croûte is only for the most dedicated cooks. I hadn't dared try one until led through each step by master chef John Clancy. Plan this dish a week in advance to have time to enjoy it. It is best made in a special pâté pan—an oblong one with removable sides. However, if you have no special hinged pâté mold, a regular long, narrow loaf pan will do. Take special care in removing the pâté.

Remember that pâté en croûte is made for appearance—the crust isn't meant to be eaten. When placing the pastry into the pan, allow enough to lay flat. Never pull it as it will rip. Work it gently. It often responds best if made and left, wrapped, at room temperature for an hour or two before rolling. Save pieces of the pastry after rolling to make pretty flowers around the cut vents. (Serves 12-14)

Utensils

1	pâté mold with hinged sides	1	funnel
2	cookie sheets with sides (jelly-roll pan)	1	rack for baking (use cake cooling rack)
2	pastry tube tips	1	rolling pin

Ingredients

Stuffing Mixture
Prepare at least 3 days before baking and 5 days before serving.

⅔	cup finely chopped shallots	4	teaspoons salt
1	large clove garlic, finely chopped	½	teaspoon freshly ground pepper
1¼	pounds (about 500 g) lean pork, ground (see note below)	½	teaspoon allspice
1¼	pounds (about 500 g) lean veal, ground	½	teaspoon thyme
1¼	pounds (about 500 g) pork fat, ground	1	bay leaf
		1	cup pistachios, shelled
3	eggs, lightly beaten		Pastry for two 2-crust pies
½	cup cognac	1	egg yolk for brushing pastry

Lining Mixture

1	pound (500 g) lean veal, cut into strips, or thin slices of cooked, pickled tongue		Cognac
		1	pound (500 g) fat back

Method

Combine all of the stuffing ingredients together and allow them to sit, covered, in the refrigerator for at least 3 days. Soak the veal or tongue in cognac for 3 days.

Have the butcher slice the fat back very thinly, then pound it to ⅛-inch thickness between waxed paper.

Assembly

Prepare at least one day in advance. Make pastry as you normally do. If using a machine, use a bread paddle for the mixing.

Roll the pastry to less than ¼-inch thickness between 2 sheets of waxed paper. Line the pâté mold with pastry. Fit it well and carefully, leaving some pastry hanging over the edge to hold the top piece. Brush with egg yolk wash. Line the pastry with half the prepared fat back.

Lay a half inch of the stuffing mixture over the fat back, using an icing knife dipped in cold water. Spread the thin strips of marinated veal or tongue. Top with stuffing, then tongue, then stuffing, until the mixture measures 2 inches above the top of the mold.

Place the final layer of fat back and pastry over top and brush with egg yolk wash to seal it. Slice off excess pastry.

Decorate

Make two circular holes in the lid using the tip of an icing bag. Make sure that the fat back is removed along with the pastry. Fit funnel into the holes so that the fat doesn't escape onto the pastry. Mark the pastry with fine lines with a sharp knife. Make pastry flowers and leaves from scraps of pastry, sticking them on with beaten egg white. Brush all over surface with egg yolk wash. Place on a rack on a jellyroll baking sheet so that any fat escaping will be caught.

Bake at 350°F for 2 hours. Test with a meat thermometer for certainty—the internal temperature should reach 170°F.

Remove from the oven and baking sheet. Place the mold and rack on another pan or remove drippings from original pan, clean and replace pan. Cool completely, until slightly cooler than your hand.

Have the aspic mixture ready (see next page). It should be semi-jelled, or slightly syrupy. Using a funnel, pour the aspic through the holes. It should take up the space between the pastry and the meat—where the meat has shrunk. Refrigerate.

When the aspic has set, remove the mold. Use a sharp knife to loosen the sides. Remove the bottom first and place the pastry bottom on the serving plate. Then, remove the sides.

Breathe a sigh of relief.

Garnish with extra chopped aspic. Chefs pour the aspic onto a jellyroll pan to set and then cube or chop it as decoration. Use watercress and lemon flowers or wedges on the tray. Always remove one or two slices and lay on the tray for serving.

Note: For those of you who can only buy meat by the kilogram the amounts may seem incongruous. For example, 1¼ pounds ground beef can read 550 g in one recipe and 600 g in another. Exactly, 1¼ pounds is 566 g. The question that is posed for a recipe writer who is not testing recipes using both systems is whether or not to round down to 500 or up to 600 grams. In this case I have chosen to use the lower figure because the higher amount will give a pâté that is too heavy.

Quick Aspic

Ingredients

½	cup egg whites (2–3)	2	sprigs parsley
6	egg shells	5	packages (8 g) gelatin
1	ripe tomato, chopped	5	cups of canned beef and
1	large Spanish onion, chopped		chicken broth, mixed
1	carrot, peeled and chopped		

Method

Beat egg whites until just frothy. Add broken egg shells and vegetables. Add 5 packages of gelatin. Place broth in a pan and heat. Add egg white mixture. Heat to boiling slowly. Turn heat off and let rest for 10 minutes.

Meanwhile, line a strainer with a clean towel. Gently ladle broth through. Pour into a low-sided pan (jellyroll pan) and cool at room temperature. To chill for pouring, place over ice cubes and stir until syrupy. Refrigerate to gel.

Emergency recipe: If the pastry develops holes after cooling, seal them with softened butter.

Late Day Pâté

Allow one hour between arriving home and serving this quick pâté. (Serves 4-6)

Ingredients

½	pound (225 g) smooth liver paste	1	clove garlic, crushed
			Freshly ground black pepper
½	pound (225 g) coarse liver paste	1	tablespoon brandy
1	tablespoon vegetable oil	1	bay leaf
1	tablespoon lemon juice	¼	cup melted butter
			Hot toasts

Method

Remove the casing from the liver pastes and combine in a bowl. Mix in the oil, lemon juice, garlic and pepper. Mash together well and taste. Some salt may be required.

Gradually stir in the brandy. Press the mixture down well, either in the bowl or in a glazed loaf pan. Place the bay leaf on top. Pour the melted butter over and refrigerate. Serve chilled on hot toasts.

Marinated Grouper

This peppery, marinated fish looks wonderful on a buffet table as an hors d'oeuvre. Surround it with lemon wheels and watercress and slice it very thinly. It tastes exquisite. (Serves 10)

Ingredients

2	pounds (1 kg) fresh grouper fillets, leave skin on	1	tablespoon mustard seeds
4	tablespoons coarse salt	2	tablespoons sugar
2	tablespoons crushed pepper-corns	1	bunch fresh dill, chopped

Method

Mix the salt, peppercorns, mustard, sugar and dill together. Sprinkle this mixture on both sides of the grouper. Place it in a flat pan, covered with tin foil. Refrigerate for 48 hours, turning every 12 hours. Serve the mustard sauce (below) separately.

Mustard Sauce

Ingredients

1	egg yolk	1	tablespoon white vinegar
$\frac{1}{2}$	teaspoon dry mustard	$\frac{1}{4}$	teaspoon Dijon mustard
$\frac{1}{2}$	teaspoon sugar	3	ounces peanut oil

Method

Mix the first 5 ingredients, then add the oil and mix well. Season with salt, if necessary.

Escargots Bourguignon

Chef Michel Lombardi of La Fringale Restaurant came to Studio 7 to talk about snails. According to him, the best come packed in cans from France. They are evenly sized, firm but tender. This recipe may be used for stuffing shells or mushroom caps. Delicious either way.

Snail shells may be purchased for filling and reused. After using, wash them carefully with hot soapy water and rinse with vinegar. Place them in a 250°F oven to dry for 20 minutes. Store in a clean jar covered loosely.

Ingredients

¾	cup butter, softened		White pepper
1–2	tablespoons minced shallots or onions	½	teaspoon rosemary
		½	teaspoon thyme
2	cloves garlic, finely chopped	½	teaspoon marjoram
1	tablespoon parsley, minced	1	bayleaf, finely crumbled
½	teaspoon salt	24	snails

Method

Preheat oven to 450°F. Cream the above ingredients together, except the snails. Place the snail in the shell and cover completely with the butter mixture. Bake for 5–10 minutes, until the butter is bubbly and the snails are hot.

Soups

Beet and Cabbage Borscht 18
Beer Soup 19
Creamy Leek and Potato Soup 24
Goulash Soup with Dumplings 22
Fresh Pea Soup 19
Charlie Brown's Pumpkin Soup 21
Hot and Spicy Shrimp Soup 20
Yogurt, Barley and Chicken Soup 23

Beet and Cabbage Borscht

Borscht is soup, but to me, it means a whole meal in a bowl. When the vegetables are added at different times during the cooking process they retain their texture and taste. Don't be afraid to make this soup with left-over meat or bones, but do taste it and alter the seasonings after it has been cooked. (Serves 4-6)

Ingredients

4	small beets, peeled and thinly sliced
1	medium onion, chopped
½	pound (200 g) lean stewing beef, cubed, or more to taste
6	cups beef stock
1	medium carrot, peeled and sliced
1	medium potato, peeled and cubed

1	stalk celery, sliced
½	medium cabbage, grated
1	10-ounce (284 mL) can tomatoes
1	small clove garlic, peeled and chopped
2	tablespoons lemon juice (or more to taste)
	Freshly ground pepper
1½	teaspoons salt, to taste

Garnish
Dollop of sour cream or yogurt
sprinkled with fresh dill

Method

Prepare the beets and onion and add to a large pot along with the beef and beef stock. Bring to the boil then reduce the heat to simmer for about 30 minutes. Add the carrot, potato and celery and simmer for another 15 minutes. Add the cabbage and cook just until tender. Add tomatoes and garlic and heat through.

Now, get bowl and spoon ready for testing. Add lemon juice, salt and pepper, tasting all the time. The soup is perfect when the sweet taste of the beets is just *slightly* altered by the sour taste of the lemon juice. The salt and pepper will heighten the contrasting tastes.

To serve, have the soup at boiling point. Ladle some into each bowl. Garnish with a spoonful of sour cream or yogurt. Sprinkle with chopped fresh dill. If dill is not in season, use some dill seed. Remember that the cream or yogurt will alter the taste slightly and the borscht may need less salt.

Beer Soup

Unusual and creamy, this soup may be served with croutons or with slices of French bread. (Serves 6)

Ingredients

2	341 mL bottles beer or ale	4	tablespoons sour cream
2	tablespoons sugar	½	teaspoon salt
4	egg yolks		Freshly ground black pepper

Method

Put the beer or ale and sugar into a large saucepan over moderate heat. Stir with a wooden spoon until the sugar is dissolved and then bring to the boil. Remove the saucepan from the heat.

Put the egg yolks into a small bowl and beat them lightly with a fork or a whisk. Beating continuously, add the sour cream, a tablespoon at a time. Place 4 tablespoons of the hot beer into the egg-and-sour-cream mixture and stir well. Beating continuously, pour the contents of the bowl into the remaining lager. Season with salt and pepper and stir to mix.

Return the saucepan to a very low heat and, stirring constantly, cook for a few minutes until the soup thickens. Do not allow it to boil. Pour the soup into warmed bowls or a tureen and serve hot.

Fresh Pea Soup

Chicken stock in the freezer means never being without a fresh vegetable soup. Here's pea soup from Babsi's restaurant in Mississauga. You can do the same with any fresh or frozen vegetable. (Serves 4)

Ingredients

1	tablespoon butter	1½	cups chicken or veal stock
1	small onion, finely chopped	½	teaspoon sweet basil
1	slice of bacon, cut into pieces		Salt and pepper to taste
1½	cups peas, fresh and shelled or frozen and thawed		

Method

Heat butter in saucepan and sauté onion, bacon and peas. Add the stock and cook for 2–3 minutes or until peas are tender. Add basil and adjust seasoning. If you prefer smooth soup, zip it through the blender or food processor before serving. Serve with Melba toast.

Hot and Spicy Shrimp Soup

Dom Yam Gung, as it is called, is undoubtedly the most unusual and exciting taste sensation I've experienced. In Thailand, few meals begin without it. Street vendors hawk it in cubby-hole street-side restaurants and elegant hostesses use it to poach whole, freshly caught fish. Light chicken broth forms the base; lemon grass, lime peel, fish and chili paste all combine to jolt your taste buds alive. (Serves 4)

These are some typical Thai ingredients:

Lemon Grass
This is a tropical plant or citronella root common to Vietnamese, Malaysian, Indonesian and Thai cooking. The lower part of the stem, which is bulblike and resembles the white part of the green onion, is edible. The loose leaves or upper stalk are used for soup and are generally discarded. To use fresh lemon grass, remove and discard the large outer leaves and ⅔ of the stalk. Slice finely and chop. To use dried lemon grass, soak for 2 hours in hot water, drain and chop finely. One stalk fresh lemon grass is equal to one tablespoon dried. Fresh lemon grass may be available in Thai grocery stores. Dried lemon grass can be found in drug stores.

Lime Leaves
A piece of lime peel may be substituted for leaves. Make certain that there is no white membrane adhering to the skin—only the green outer peel. One strip of peel will substitute for 2 lime or lemon leaves. If you have a lemon tree as a house plant, scald the leaves and use these.

Chili Paste
This is available in Thai, Chinese or Indian grocery stores. One tablespoon is equal to 2–3 small chilies.

Straw Mushrooms
These are available in cans in Chinese or other Oriental grocery stores.

Fish Sauce
This is available in Thai grocery stores. However, you may substitute 2 teaspoons of light soy sauce combined with 1 mashed anchovy fillet for 1 tablespoon of fish sauce.

Caution: Prepare dried, fresh or canned chilies wearing rubber gloves. Never touch your face before washing your hands.

Ingredients

4	cups chicken stock, fat removed	2	tablespoons lime or lemon juice
1	stalk lemon grass (1 table-spoon dried)	2–3	small dried chilies, slivered, seeds removed (1 teaspoon chili paste)
2	pieces lime leaves (1 strip rind)	2	tablespoons coriander leaves, coarsely chopped
2	tablespoons fish sauce		
1	medium-sized raw shrimp, peeled and cleaned	3	green onions, coarsely chopped
1	cup straw mushrooms		

Method

If using dried lemon grass, soak it in ¼ cup boiling water for 2 hours as mentioned above. Heat the broth in a saucepan until boiling and add the lemon grass, lime leaves, fish sauce and shrimp. Lower the heat and simmer gently for 2 minutes. Add mushrooms, lime juice and chilies. Simmer for another 2 minutes. Remove leaves, rind and chilies. Just before serving, add coriander and green onions as garnish.

Charlie Brown's Pumpkin Soup

If Hallowe'en leaves you with leftover pumpkin pulp, this soup is a novel change. It uses leeks and potatoes—a slightly different taste than other pumpkin soups. (Makes about 6 cups)

Ingredients

¼	cup butter	1	cup cooked, mashed pumpkin
1	large onion, chopped		
2	leeks, well cleaned and chopped	2	cups chicken stock
		2	cups milk
½-1	teaspoon curry powder		Salt and freshly ground black pepper
1	large potato, peeled and diced		Fresh parsley, chopped

Method

In soup pot, melt the butter and soften onion and leeks. Stir in the curry powder and cook 1 minute. Add potato, pumpkin and chicken stock. Simmer until potato is soft.

Purée in food processor or blender until smooth. (May require two batches.) Return to soup pot and add milk, heating until very hot, but not boiling. Season to taste with salt and pepper. Serve sprinkled with chopped parsley.

Goulash Soup with Dumplings

For a perfect goulash you need Hungarian paprika. It should be bright red in color, slightly sweet to smell and should leave your mouth tingling. Top the hot soup with tiny doughy dumplings for a delectable combination. (Serves 6–8)

Ingredients

2 medium onions, finely chopped	2 large potatoes, peeled and cubed
2 tablespoons butter	
1 large clove garlic	1 cup carrot, peeled and sliced
1 teaspoon caraway seeds	1½ cups turnip, peeled and cubed
1 pound (500 g) lean stewing beef, cut into cubes	1 cup parsnip, peeled, sliced and cubed
1½ tablespoons Hungarian paprika	1 cup celery (2 stalks), sliced
¼ teaspoon cayenne pepper (use less if hot foods aren't favorites)	1 cup cauliflowerettes (1 small cauliflower, flowers sliced)
	Salt and freshly ground black pepper (optional)
6 cups beef stock	

Method

A large cast iron or heavy-bottomed copper pot is needed for this soup— so that the onions and meat will have a slow sauté.

Melt the butter over medium heat, add the minced onion and sweat, stirring constantly until they are shiny and golden yellow.

If you used a food processor for the onions, turn it on and add the garlic and caraway seeds (otherwise chop). Add the beef to the pan with the minced garlic and seeds and stir for about 10 minutes, or until the beef is lightly browned. Add the paprika and cayenne and stir. Gradually add the beef stock, cover and raise the heat until the soup begins to boil. Simmer covered for 30 minutes.

Add the potatoes, carrot, turnip and parsnip and continue to simmer the soup for another 30 minutes. Add celery and cauliflower and cook for 15 minutes more. Add salt and freshly ground pepper, tasting all the while until the soup has a full robust flavor.

Cool in the pot and transfer to a covered container for chilling. When the fat has hardened, skim it off. Reheat the soup to boiling and meanwhile mix up the dumplings. They may also be prepared ahead, as long as they are covered.

When the soup comes to the boil, drop the dumplings by spoonfuls into it. They are done when they lose their yellow color (about 7 minutes). Serve hot.

Dumplings

Ingredients

3   tablespoons all-purpose flour   1   egg
½   teaspoon salt

Method

Measure the flour into a small bowl and mix with the salt. Add the egg and mix the mixture with a fork, beating until smooth.

Cover and set aside until the soup is hot. Drop by spoonfuls into the hot soup.

Yogurt, Barley and Chicken Soup

What can I say? This is simply my favorite soup! (Makes 6 servings)

Ingredients

½   cup pearl barley, soaked over-
    night in water
2   tablespoons butter or oil
2   medium onions, chopped
    finely
5   cups chicken stock
1   cup white chicken meat,
    cooked and shredded (optional)

1   tablespoon fresh parsley,
    finely chopped
½   teaspoon salt
    Pinch of white ground pepper
1   container (500 g) plain yogurt
1   tablespoon fresh mint, chopped
    (use half the amount if using
    dried)

Method

Before going to bed, measure the barley and cover with cold water to soak. Next day drain through a sieve. In a heavy-bottomed saucepan heat the butter or oil and add the onions. Stir over medium heat with a wooden spoon until the onions are softened, golden yellow and shiny (about 7 minutes). Add the stock and bring to a boil.

Reduce the heat, add the barley, cover and simmer for half an hour. Add the parsley, chicken, salt and pepper and continue to simmer for 10 minutes.

This may be prepared ahead of time up to this point. When ready to serve, pour the yogurt into a bowl and gradually add the hot soup. Stir constantly so that the yogurt will not separate. Return the pot to the stove and heat gently until very hot. Add the mint and serve.

Creamy Leek and Potato Soup

(Serves 6)

Ingredients

4	tablespoons butter	2	cups water
2	cups white leeks, trimmed, washed and sliced	1	tablespoon salt
		½	teaspoon white pepper
1	cup onions, sliced	1	cup milk
3	medium-sized potatoes (about 1 pound — 500 g)	¾	cup cream
			Diced croutons
4	cups chicken broth		

Method

Melt the butter in a deep saucepan, add the prepared leeks and onions. Cook over a low flame, stirring constantly for 10 minutes, until vegetables are soft but not brown. Add potatoes, chicken broth and water. Season with salt and pepper. Bring to the boil, cover with lid, reduce heat and simmer for 1 hour.

Blend in the milk, simmer for 5 minutes. Strain through sieve or food mill, or purée in blender. Check seasoning. Before serving, stir in the cream and reheat for 5 minutes. Serve with diced croutons on side.

Diced Croutons

Cut 3 slices of white bread into ¾ inch cubes (about 1½ cups). Melt 1–2 tablespoons butter in a skillet, brown bread cubes on all sides. Drain on paper towels.

BEEF, PORK, VEAL AND LAMB

BEEF

Meat Glaze 28
Cross Rib Roast 26
Pot Roast with Crabapples 27
Spiced Short Ribs 28
Marinade #1 29
Marinade #2 30
Beef and Vegetable Stew 30
Hot Meat and Rice Salad 33
Beef Steak and Kidney Pie 31
Ground Beef Facts 31
Pepper Steak 35
Little Hot Meatballs 34
Crusty Beef and Vegetable Pie 37
Carefree Casserole 36
Janet's Heart Soup 38

PORK

Pork Rolls with Mushroom
and Ham Filling 40
Breaded Pork Chops 43
Pork and Fruit Casserole 40
Pork and Lemon Casserole 39
Chinese Ribs 42
Chinese Pork and Pineapple 42
Pork and Vegetable Salad 44

VEAL

Veal Birds Jardinière 44

LAMB

Lamb M'shwi 45
Noisettes of Lamb with
Basil Cream Sauce 46

Know the Cuts

1. Round
2. Sirloin Tip
3. Rump
4. Sirloin
5. Porterhouse
6. T-Bone
7. Wing
8. Tenderloin or Filet
9. Rib
10. Short Ribs (Braising Ribs)
11. Blade
12. Chuck Short Rib
13. Cross Rib
14. Shoulder
15. Neck (generally cut into Stewing Beef)
16. Brisket (may be ground)
17. Plate (may be ground)
18. Flank
19. Shank
20. Shank

Most tender

Medium tender

Less tender

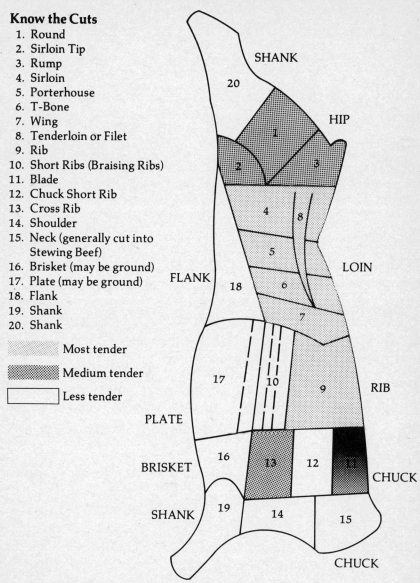

Courtesy of Beef Information Centre, Toronto, Calgary, Vancouver.

Cross Rib Roast

The cross rib roast comes from the most exercised part of the animal—the shoulder; therefore, it needs special care. Many customers mistakenly buy it as a quick oven roast and curse the butcher because it is tough after cooking.

The accompanying diagram shows where it is situated and why it cannot be simply roasted but rather must be marinated or cooked, covered, with moisture for a long time at a low temperature.

When offered at a special price, I buy a large cross rib roast and cut it myself into ribs for a short rib stew, marinated steaks and a pot roast.

Removing the bones before cooking solves the difficult problem of carving at the table. It also provides more servings and less waste.

Cut the string from the meat and remove or cut off the bones. Marinate them for barbecuing (see ps. 29, 30 for marinades) or set them aside for a pot roast. Cut a couple or more steaks and marinate these. The remainder can be prepared as a pot roast, for instance, one with crab apples (see below). It was a hit with our crew!

For three meals I suggest a 5–6 pound (2.5–3 kg) roast for 4 people or a 3–4 pound (1.5–2 kg) roast for 2.

Pot Roast with Crab Apples
(Serves 6)

Ingredients

3–4	tablespoons flour		1	28-ounce jar (769 mL) spiced crab apples
1½	teaspoons salt			
¼	teaspoon pepper		2	tablespoons lemon juice
¼	teaspoon ground allspice		½	cup raisins
3	pounds (1.5 kg) chuck, cross rib or pot roast		2	tablespoons all-purpose flour
2	tablespoons lard or margarine		½	cup cold water

Method

Mix flour, salt, pepper and allspice and dredge meat with the mixture. Brown meat on all sides in the lard in heavy kettle or Dutch oven. Drain crab apples, reserving juice. Add enough water to juice to make 1 cup. Add to meat with lemon juice. Put rack under meat. Cover and simmer for 3 hours, or until tender. About 15 minutes before meat is done, add crab apples and raisins.

To serve, remove meat and crab apples to platter. Blend 2 table-spoons flour with the cold water and add to pan liquid, stirring. Add a little more water if necessary to make the right consistency of gravy. Let boil a few minutes. Slice meat, garnish with crab apples and serve with the gravy.

Spiced Short Ribs

(Serves 4–6)

Ingredients

2½–3	pounds (1.5 kg) chuck short ribs or ribs cut from a cross rib roast)	½	cup dried apricots (optional)
		2	tablespoons sugar
	Salt, pepper and flour	½	teaspoon cinnamon
2	tablespoons shortening, butter or margarine	⅛	teaspoon ground cloves
		¼	teaspoon ground allspice
1	cup water	3	tablespoons vinegar
1	cup pitted prunes		

Method

Season meat with salt, pepper and sprinkling of flour. Brown on all sides in the shortening in large, heavy kettle or Dutch oven. Remove meat and pour off fat. Place meat back in pot. Add the water, bring to boil, cover and simmer 1½ hours. Add prunes, apricots and mixture of remaining ingredients. Simmer, adding more water if necessary, one hour longer, or until very tender.

Meat Glaze

If there is a secret to good cooking beyond the mastery of taste and technique, it is here, in this recipe. Watery sauces and tasteless entrées are a thing of the past once you have cubes of meat glaze in the freezer. They should be made over a period of two days; the resulting concentrate may be stored in the freezer for 6 months.

Dissolve a cube in a quart of water and you have soup stock, add a bit of glaze to the pan after you sauté chops or breast of chicken and the result is a heavenly, unforgettable flavor. (Makes 12 cubes)

Ingredients

10–15	pounds (4.5–7 kg) meat scraps, bones and fat (Try to include some beef or veal shin bones and chicken feet if available)	2	large stalks celery, chopped
		6	sprigs parsley
			Pinch of thyme
		¼	teaspoon savory
2	large onions, sliced	2	bay leaves
2	large carrots, peeled and sliced	12	whole peppercorns
			Cold water

Method

Preheat oven to 375°F. Brown the scraps and bones in a roasting pan in oven for one hour, turning several times. Add the sliced onions and carrots to the pan and cook for a further 30 minutes until brown.

Transfer meat scraps and vegetables to a large stockpot that will hold about 20 quarts (20 L). Carefully collect the meat sediment and juices from the roasting pan and add to the stockpot. Add the remaining ingredients and cover with cold water. Bring to the boil, cover, reduce heat and simmer for 4 hours.

Strain the broth into a 12-quart (12 L) saucepan using a strainer lined with damp cheesecloth. Cool quickly. Place in refrigerator overnight to settle.

Next day, carefully remove hardened fat from the top of the broth and discard. Bring to the boil and cook uncovered over high heat until reduced to about a pint. Glaze will turn dark and syrupy. This may take from one to two hours. Remove dividers from ice cube tray and pour in the glaze. Place in refrigerator for 6 hours or so. Remove meat glaze from tray by easing up one end and slipping it out. Cut into cubes. Store cubes in a plastic bag or container in the freezer until required.

Marinade #1

(Serves 4)

Ingredients

1-2	pounds (500 g-1 kg) beef	2	tablespoons Worcestershire sauce
1	cup ketchup	1	tablespoon *each* brown sugar and prepared mustard
½	cup water		
¼	cup wine vinegar	1	teaspoon chili powder
2	tablespoons dry onion soup mix	½	teaspoon salt

Method

Combine marinade ingredients and heat to boiling. Pour marinade over beef and coat all sides. Marinate at least 1 hour in refrigerator. Drain. Barbecue on spit or roast in oven, basting frequently.

Remove from grill onto a carving board. Carve the meat on the bias, across the grain into one-inch thick slices. Heat marinade and serve as sauce over sliced beef.

Marinade #2

(Serves 4)

Ingredients

1-2	pounds (500 g-1 kg) beef	2	tablespoons chopped chives or green onions
1	7½-ounce can (213 mL) tomato sauce	¼	teaspoon *each* garlic powder, salt, celery salt
2	tablespoons gin	½	teaspoon pepper

Method

Combine marinade ingredients and pour over beef. Marinate 3-4 hours in refrigerator, turning meat occasionally. Drain, but save marinade. Pat meat dry. Broil. Heat marinade mixture to just under boiling. Slice meat across grain into thin slices and serve with marinade sauce.

Beef and Vegetable Stew

If you are counting calories, omit browning the meat first. Just combine everything and simmer. If the sauce looks pale after the vegetables go in, brown the flour in a hot pan for a minute or two before mixing. This is a colorful stew as well as a tasty one. (Serves 4)

Ingredients

3	tablespoons vegetable oil	1	medium acorn squash, peeled and cubed
2	pounds (1 kg) stewing beef, cubed	1	12-ounce (340 g) package frozen lima beans
3	medium onions, sliced	3	tablespoons flour
1	teaspoon salt	⅓	cup water
1	teaspoon dried thyme	1	cup cherry tomatoes
¼	teaspoon pepper		
1½	cups beef bouillon or water		

Method

In a large casserole or Dutch oven, brown stewing beef in oil. Add onions and lightly brown. Stir in salt, thyme, pepper and bouillon. Cover and simmer 1½ hours.

Add squash and lima beans, simmer 15 minutes or until tender. In a jar with a tight-fitting lid, combine flour and water. Shake well. Stir into casserole to thicken gravy. Just before serving, gently stir in tomatoes. Heat slightly and serve.

Beef Steak and Kidney Pie

An old favorite returns. Use frozen, prepared pastry or your own home-made. The pastry stretches the meat and add wonders to the flavor. (Serves 6–8)

Ingredients

1	pound (500 g) chuck steak, cubed	2	cups hot water	
1	pound (500 g) beef kidney, cleaned	1	teaspoon salt	
		½	teaspoon pepper	
½	cup browned flour (stir over heat until golden)	1	teaspoon dry mustard	
		½	teaspoon ginger	
2	tablespoons oil		Pinch cinnamon	
3	medium onions, sliced	1	cup cold water	
			Pastry	

Method

Dice kidney and steak, then roll in browned flour. Set aside remaining browned flour. Heat oil in a large frying pan, add floured meat. Cook until all meat is seared. Add onions and stir until blended. Add hot water, salt, pepper and seasonings. Bring to a boil, stirring all the time.

Cover and simmer over low heat until kidney and steak are tender or use a pressure cooker for 15 minutes at 15-pound pressure. Drain the meat, saving the liquid. Combine remaining flour with the cold water, add hot liquid from the meat and blend. Return to the pan, stir until thickened and the flour has cooked (about 10 minutes). Place the meat and thickened gravy in a 1½ quart (1.5 L) casserole, cover with pastry and make small slits in the top. Bake at 400°F for 40 minutes.

Ground Beef Facts

Pinching pennies by using ground beef has been an accepted kitchen practice ever since our ancestors put cleaver to tough beef on a chopping block and found that it was easier to chew. But there are ways of pinching those pennies even harder. Read these pointers from the Beef Information Centre.

Ground beef is exactly what its name indicates—beef that has been mechanically ground to make it more tender. The grinding action breaks down the connective tissues of less tender cuts to make the meat easy to chew and quick to cook.

Ground beef may come from any part of the carcass, but generally comes from the plate, neck, brisket, flank or shank.

New government regulations state that all ground beef be labelled as either "minced" or "ground" beef and not as "hamburg". From now on, hamburg will refer only to cooked ground beef.

These regulations also require that ground beef be labelled according to its fat content. The three fat-level categories are as follows:

• Regular "ground" or "minced" beef to contain no more than 30% fat.

• Medium ground beef to contain no more than 23% fat.

• Lean ground beef to contain no more than 17% fat.

Shopping for Ground Beef

Choose the ground beef that will provide you with the right amount of fat for the particular dish you are making. For example, buy regular ground beef for hamburgers or patties. This will supply enough fat for self-basting and allows the patties to be juicy, flavorful and not too firm in texture.

Buy medium or lean ground beef for casseroles or meat loaf. This amount of fat gives a firmer product and does not drain too much fat. However, if ground beef is cooked and drained before being added to a casserole, regular ground beef is suitable.

Cost Comparison

To compare the cost of the three ground beef categories, we know that regular ground beef contains 70% lean, medium contains 77% lean and lean contains 83% lean.

Categories	Avg. Cost/lb.	Lean Portion	Lean Cost/lb.
Regular	$1.28	.70	($1.28/.70) or $1.83
Medium	$1.68	.77	($1.68/.77) or $2.18
Lean	$1.98	.83	($1.98/.83) or $2.39

So, you can save half your beef dollar by buying regular ground beef for casserole and meatball recipes.

Don't be disturbed if the inside of the ground beef package is dark red while the outside is bright red. The difference in color is due to oxidation. Oxygen from the air has brightened the beef on the outside, but it could not reach the beef on the inside. It is illegal to add colorings to ground beef.

Care and Storage

Ground beef is handled more during processing and packaging than other cuts of beef, so there is greater concern about levels of bacteria. However, if the beef is handled properly after it leaves the store, there is no need to worry.

At the store
Make sure the package is properly wrapped. Check the label to find out if the ground beef has been previously frozen. See that the beef is placed in its own bag to help keep it insulated. Get it home as quickly as possible so that it does not get too warm in the car.

At home
If you plan to use the ground beef within 2 days, keep it stored in the coldest part of the refrigerator. It may remain in the store wrapping. If it is to be kept longer, remove it from the store wrapping and rewrap it tightly in proper freezer paper, to prevent loss of moisture and freezer burn. It may then be frozen and stored for up to 3 months. Make sure all packages are labelled with the date, fat level (30%, 23% or 17%) and weight or number of portions. When thawing ground beef, it is best to do so in the refrigerator, so that if it is thawed a few hours before being cooked, it is still kept cool. Allow about 4–7 hours per pound to thaw in the refrigerator and 2 hours per pound at room temperature. Cook as soon as it has thawed and avoid refreezing thawed beef unless there are ice crystals present. If it must be refrozen, it should be cooked first, then may be frozen. Cooked ground beef dishes may be frozen for 2–3 months if well wrapped. Slightly undercook, before freezing, so that in reheating, the casserole, etc., will not be overcooked. Reheat directly from the frozen state to help prevent bacterial growth during thawing.

Hot Meat and Rice Salad

A quick and delicious supper that is economical, too. The mayonnaise adds a different touch. (Makes 4 servings)

Ingredients

½	pound (225 g) lean ground beef	1	cup sliced celery
1	teaspoon garlic salt	½	cup chopped green peppers
⅛	teaspoon Tobasco sauce	½	cup chopped onions
1	tablespoon lemon juice	2	tomatoes, cut into eighths
½	cup mayonnaise	½	cup crushed corn chips
1½	cups cooked rice		

Method

Cook meat in a hot skillet until browned; drain off the fat. Add garlic salt, Tobasco sauce and lemon juice to mayonnaise. Stir into meat mixture with rice, celery, green peppers, onions and tomatoes. Cover pan, reduce heat and continue cooking at low heat for 20 minutes. Remove lid and add corn chips. Serve.

Little Hot Meatballs

These were tested on a group of teenagers and received raves. Some even asked for more hot peppers! (Serves 6)

Ingredients

1½ pounds (700 g) minced beef
1 large onion, finely chopped
1 red pepper, seeded and chopped
½ cup rice, soaked in cold water for 30 minutes and drained

1 teaspoon salt
½ teaspoon black pepper
1 tablespoon paprika
1 large egg, lightly beaten

Sauce

1 14-ounce (398 mL) can peeled tomatoes
1 onion, coarsely chopped
1 celery stalk, trimmed and chopped
4 tablespoons tomato ketchup

1 tablespoon soft brown sugar
1 teaspoon salt
½ teaspoon black pepper
½ teaspoon dried thyme
1 bay leaf
1 cup milk
Pinch cayenne pepper

Method

Sauce

Place tomatoes with juice, onion, celery, ketchup, sugar, salt, pepper, thyme and bay leaf in a large pan. Pour in the milk. Place over moderate heat and bring the mixture to the boil, stirring frequently. Reduce the heat to low, cover and simmer the sauce for 30 minutes.

Meanwhile, prepare the meatballs. In a large mixing bowl, combine all the ingredients together until they are thoroughly mixed. Form into about 16 balls, approximately 2 inches in diameter. Set aside.

Remove the pan from the heat. Pour the sauce through a fine wire strainer set over a medium-sized bowl. Remove and discard bay leaf. Using the back of a wooden spoon, rub the cooked vegetables through the strainer until only a dry pulp is left. Discard the pulp. Return the sauce to the pan and reheat. Stir in the cayenne and add the meatballs. Increase the heat to high and bring the mixture to the boil. Reduce the heat to low, cover, and simmer for 40–45 minutes or until the meatballs are cooked. Serve at once.

Pepper Steak

The secret to a full-bodied steak or hamburger isn't the meat alone, but its combination with a wonderful reduced sauce called meat glaze. Follow this recipe for pepper steak, using either the best fillet steak or simple hamburger. Then serve it to the fussiest guest. Raves are guaranteed. (Serves 4)

Ingredients

1	tablespoon dry mustard	4	tablespoons cognac
2	tablespoons white or black peppercorns (white are hotter)	3	tablespoons cereal or 35% cream
4	fillet steaks or hamburgers Vegetable oil	1	cup meat glaze (see p. 28) Salt, if desired
4	tablespoons clarified butter (see below)		

Method

Combine the dry mustard and peppercorns on a wooden board and crush them with a rolling pin. Spread the steak or burgers with vegetable oil and then coat each with the crushed pepper. Heat a heavy sauté pan. While it is heating, set aside 2 tablespoons clarified butter and the cream. These and the meat glaze should be ready after cooking the meat.

Add 2 tablespoons clarified butter and 1 tablespoon vegetable oil to the hot pan and add the beef. It should lie flat in the pan and not touch the sides. Cook until dark brown on one side then turn. Allow 1½ minutes on each side and then reduce the heat and cook a further 1 minute (for rare meat).

Remove meat to a hot plate. Add cognac immediately and scrape the pan of drippings. Immediately add the glaze and allow it to reduce to half. Reduce heat, add the cream, stir gently; then add the butter, 1 tablespoon at a time. Pour over meat. Taste and adjust seasoning. Serve immediately.

Clarified Butter

Melt butter over medium heat, remove and allow to stand at room temperature for a few minutes so that the milk solids settle to the bottom. Skim the butter fat from the top and store in a covered jar in the refrigerator.

Carefree Casserole

Oh, how I long for a repertoire of delicious meal-in-a-dish recipes. Not those that call for gobs of homemade stock or cooked rice or dried saffron. Just simple meat and vegetable casseroles that I can prepare for someone else to bake on those nights when cooking is the *last* thing I want to do.

Here is one—a casserole that uses *uncooked* noodles! (Serves 6–8)

Ingredients

1	pound (500 g) ground beef		Pinch dried thyme
2	medium onions, sliced	½	teaspoon dried marjoram
1	clove garlic, chopped	1	teaspoon Worcestershire sauce
2	cans (540 mL each) tomatoes	½	teaspoon Tabasco sauce
3	tablespoons tomato paste	8	ounces (225 g) uncooked broad noodles
1	cup water		
½	teaspoon Hungarian paprika	¼	cup grated Parmesan cheese
1	bay leaf		

Method

Heat a sauté pan until very hot and then add the beef. Stir to separate the meat and continue cooking on high until browned. If there is excess fat in the pan, drain it off. Reduce the heat. Add the onions and garlic to the meat, cover and simmer for 2 minutes. Add all of the ingredients except the noodles and Parmesan cheese. Stir to mix, cover and simmer for 5 minutes.

In a 2½ quart (2.5 L) soufflé pan or casserole, layer the sauce and noodles beginning and ending with the sauce. Bake at 375°F for 45 minutes. Sprinkle with the cheese and bake for another 5 minutes. Serve hot.

Microwave Instructions

Cook the ground beef in a 2-quart glass casserole for 3–4 minutes on Full Power, stirring twice to break up the meat during cooking. Drain off excess fat. Add onions and garlic and cook an additional 1–2 minutes on Full Power. Add all of the ingredients, except noodles and Parmesan cheese. Cook 4–5 minutes on Full Power, stirring occasionally.

In a 2½-quart microwave soufflé dish or casserole, layer sauce and noodles beginning and ending with the sauce. Bake uncovered for 5 minutes on Full Power. Rotate the dish if necessary and bake for 10–15 minutes on Medium (50% Power) until noodles are tender. Sprinkle with the cheese and let stand for 5–10 minutes before serving.

Crusty Beef and Vegetable Pie

Here is ground beef surrounded by lots of vegetables and raisins with a topping of cheese and toast that is thick and crusty. You can whip some potatoes and use them for a top crust but this crust avoids the time-consuming and messy step of peeling, cooking and mashing potatoes. It's hearty so a salad is all that's called for. You'll have two egg whites left over—they are great in Lemon and Strawberry Sherbet or simply added for frothier scrambled eggs. (Serves 4–6)

Ingredients

2	tablespoons vegetable oil	1/4	teaspoon freshly ground black pepper
1	medium-sized onion, sliced		
1	clove garlic, chopped finely	1	14-ounce can (398 mL) carrots, drained
1	pound (500 g) lean ground beef		
1/2	pound (250 g) zucchini, thinly sliced	1	8-ounce can (227 mL) baked beans
1/4	cup raisins	1	12-ounce can (341 mL) corn, drained
1/2	teaspoon salt		

Topping

10	slices French bread, cubed, soaked in 2 egg yolks with 2 cups milk	1	cup grated Cheddar or Swiss cheese
			Freshly grated pepper

Method

Heat the oil in a large, deep frying pan that will be able to go under the broiler. Add the onion and sauté for 7 minutes; then add the garlic. Continue over medium-low heat until they are soft and golden but not brown. Remove with a slotted spoon to a bowl. Wipe the pan with paper towel. Heat the pan and add the beef. Sauté until the redness disappears. Lift the meat with a slotted spoon and drain the fat remaining in the pan.

Add the meat, onions and garlic back to the pan and keep on medium heat. Add the sliced zucchini, raisins, salt and pepper. If you have any other quick-cooking vegetables such as green beans, celery or broccoli, slice them finely and add. Cover the pan and simmer until the vegetables are done—no longer than 15 minutes.

Meanwhile, open vegetable cans, drain the liquid from the carrots and corn into a jar to hold for a vegetable soup. Add them to the pan and heat through. Remove the pan from the heat. Set aside. If using later, cover the pan and reheat just before broiling.

Place soaked bread cubes over the casserole, sprinkle with cheese and pepper. Place under the broiler about 3 inches below the heat. Broil until crisp and brown.

Janet's Heart Soup

Pierre and Janet Berton celebrated Canada's Centenary in 1967 by bringing all of their favorite recipes together, along with classic Canadian recipes, in their book *Canadian Food Guide*. The indisputable hit of the book was Janet's Heart Soup. Serves as many as you want for as long as two weeks.

Ingredients

1	large beef heart	1	teaspoon celery seed
4	quarts (4 L) cold water	1	teaspoon marjoram
	Leaves and tops from 4 stalks	1	teaspoon thyme
	of celery	1	teaspoon basil
3	large onions, finely chopped	½	teaspoon sage
4	celery stalks, finely diced	½	teaspoon savory
2	carrots, finely diced	½	teaspoon rosemary
½	turnip, finely diced	½	teaspoon chervil
¼	green pepper, finely diced		Dash Tabasco sauce
¼	cup parsley, finely diced		Dash Worcestershire sauce
½	cup chives, finely diced		Dash Angostura Bitters
2	large cans (540 mL) tomatoes		Salt and pepper to taste
1	teaspoon oregano		

Method

Place the beef heart in a large pot with the water, bring to a boil and skim. Add the celery leafs and tops with the onions and simmer with the heart, covered for 2 days. Remove the meat and vegetables and strain the broth. To the strained broth add all of the vegetables, herbs and seasonings, simmer together for half an hour and serve with a little dry bread; this is a meal in itself.

For future meals remove all vegetables, discard and strain again. Then add ½ cup each of diced celery, carrots and onions. Bring to the boil, but don't cook the vegetables any further. Serve. The soup improves with age. As it simmers on the back of the stove the water in which other vegetables have been cooked may be added to it. If this makes the stock too thick, simply strain and start again.

To use the beef heart, grind it and make shepherd's pie, or stuff it with breadcrumbs, onions, celery and all of the herbs and spices listed for the soup. Bake at 325°F for ½ hour and serve with baked potatoes.

Pork and Lemon Casserole

This is a simple top-of-the-stove dinner that combines the warm flavors of pork and celery with the tart taste of lemon. Our tasters agreed that it was delicious. A plain steamed rice tossed with green beans or peas makes a perfect accompaniment. (Serves 6–8)

Ingredients

3	pounds (1.5 kg) pork butt, trimmed and cut into small cubes	3¾	cups chicken stock	
		1	teaspoon dried marjoram	
¼	cup all-purpose flour	1	teaspoon dried chervil	
½	teaspoon salt	½	teaspoon dried thyme	
¼	teaspoon black pepper, ground		Juice and rind from 2 lemons	
¼	cup vegetable oil	2	lemons, rind and pith removed, then cubed	
3	medium-sized onions, chopped	2	tomatoes, diced	
2	garlic cloves, crushed	½	tablespoon butter or margarine	
4	stalks celery, cut into the same size as the pork	½	tablespoon all-purpose flour	

Method

Toss the pork cubes with the flour, salt and pepper. In a large sauté pan that has a lid heat the oil and, when it is hot add the onions. Cook them, stirring until they turn golden and translucent. Add the garlic and cook for an additional two minutes. Remove the onions and garlic with a slotted spoon to a plate and reheat the oil. Add the pork cubes and allow to sear for about 5 minutes, or until they are browned. Remove them to the plate as well.

Add the celery and chicken stock. Bring to the boil, add the pork, onions and garlic and lower the heat to simmer. Add the herbs along with the pieces of lemon rind and juice. Cover the pan. Simmer for one hour.

Remove the lemon rind from the casserole and discard it. Make sure that there is no white membrane or pith remaining in the other 2 lemons. Remove each segment from the centre and then chop each segment into three pieces. Add these and the tomato pieces. Increase the heat so that the sauce begins to boil.

Meanwhile, combine the butter and flour together into a smooth paste. Using a whisk, drop the paste by teaspoons into the hot liquid, blending constantly with the whisk. Reduce the heat and stir for a couple of minutes—the sauce will thicken. Remove from the stove and serve.

Pork and Fruit Casserole

(Makes 6 servings)

Ingredients

16	pitted prunes, halved	½	teaspoon black pepper
16	dried apricots, halved	1	teaspoon dried sage
½	teaspoon allspice	2	tablespoons butter
	Juice and grated rind of	1	tablespoon vegetable oil
	½ orange	1	tablespoon brown sugar
	Juice and grated rind of	1	clove garlic, minced
	½ lemon	2	large apples, peeled, cored
1	cup dry white wine		and sliced
4–5	pound (2–2.5 kg) loin of	2	teaspoons cornstarch
	pork, boned and rolled	½	cup apple juice

Method

The night before, place dried prunes and apricots in a bowl. Add allspice, orange rind and juice, lemon rind and juice and white wine. Stir to combine and soak overnight, covered.

The following day, rub pork on all sides with pepper and sage. In a large casserole or Dutch oven, brown pork in butter and oil. Pour soaked fruit mixture over pork. Sprinkle on brown sugar and garlic, cover and simmer 2 hours, basting frequently. Skim off fat. Add sliced apples and cook 20 minutes longer. Remove roast to warm platter.

Mix cornstarch and apple juice. Stir in pan juices. Cook until thickened. Slice pork and serve topped with fruit gravy.

Pork Rolls with Mushroom and Ham Filling

With everyone cost conscious today, it's encouraging to see that butchers are responding with inexpensive alternatives to costly cuts of meat. This dish is usually prepared using veal schnitzel but it is much too expensive now. We tried substituting the very thin pork schnitzel and were delighted with the results. Make it ahead and refrigerate until baking time. (Serves 6)

Ingredients

2	pounds (1 kg) pork schnitzel, pounded thin, all visible fat removed	½	cup Swiss cheese, grated

Sauce

2	tablespoons vegetable oil	1	19-ounce can (540 mL) tomatoes
2	medium onions, thinly sliced	½	teaspoon salt
1	large clove garlic, finely chopped	1	teaspoon black pepper
2	teaspoons fresh parsley, chopped	3	tablespoons grated Parmesan cheese

Filling

½	cup butter	¼	teaspoon nutmeg
16-18	mushrooms, wiped clean and finely chopped	2	tablespoons dry bread-crumbs
½	cup finely chopped ham	2	tablespoons chicken stock or white wine
½	teaspoon salt		
1	teaspoon black pepper		

Method

Sauce
In a large saucepan, cook onion and garlic in oil over medium heat for 5-7 minutes. Add parsley, tomatoes, salt and pepper. Bring to the boil. Simmer gently for 30 minutes. Remove from heat and stir in Parmesan cheese.

Filling
Sauté mushrooms and ham in 2 tablespoons butter. Add salt, pepper, nutmeg, breadcrumbs and stock (or wine).

Assembly
Lay pork pieces on flat surface. Divide the filling evenly among them. Roll up and secure with toothpicks or string. Melt remaining butter in skillet. Brown pork rolls carefully on all sides, cooking for 8-10 minutes. Transfer pork rolls to casserole dish. Pour sauce over meat. Bake at 350°F for 45-50 minutes. Remove toothpicks or string. Sprinkle with Swiss cheese. Bake until cheese is melted—about 5 minutes.

Microwave Instructions

Prepare the recipe following the directions above until the meat is rolled and secured with a toothpick. Melt the remaining butter in a large ceramic casserole. Brown the pork rolls carefully on all sides, cooking for 8-10 minutes. Drain off the excess fat and pour the sauce over the meat. Cover and bake 5 minutes on Full Power. Rearrange and turn rolls over and bake 10-12 minutes on Medium (50% Power) until tender. Remove toothpicks or string. Sprinkle with Swiss cheese and let stand 5-10 minutes, covered, before serving.

Chinese Ribs

Here is an ideal recipe for ribs. Placing them in the microwave oven or steaming them before the final baking makes them much less fat. (Serves 4)

Ingredients

4	pounds (2 kg) spare ribs (slice off flank, peel off membrane, trim fat)	Honey mixed with a bit of mustard for glaze

Marinade

1	tablespoon ketchup		Dash of ginger powder
2	tablespoons hot ketchup		Dash of garlic salt
2	tablespoons hoisin sauce (can be interchanged with plum sauce)	1-2	tablespoons dark soy sauce
		½	teaspoon sesame oil
1	tablespoon sherry	½	teaspoon 5-spice powder (see p. 164 for homemade variety)
1	tablespoon sugar		

Method

Steam, microwave, or boil the ribs for 5–10 minutes. Wipe dry with paper towel. Score ribs diagonally, rub marinade over them, then marinate 3–8 hours.

Preheat oven to 375°F. Place ribs on top of the oven broiler pan and put water in the bottom. Bake for 25–30 minutes per side or until meat starts to pull, then turn. When done, glaze with honey mixture, cook 5 minutes more, then serve.

Chinese Pork and Pineapple

(Serves 4)

Ingredients

2	tablespoons vegetable oil	1	can (284 mL) pineapple bits, drained	
1	medium green pepper, cut in thin strips	1	tablespoon cornstarch	
2	stalks celery, sliced		Sugar	
2	green onions, cut into 1-inch lengths		Salt	
		½	teaspoon powdered ginger	
1	can (199 mL) water chestnuts, drained, rinsed and sliced	½	cup chicken stock	
		2	teaspoons lemon juice	
1	cup sliced mushrooms (canned will do)	1½	tablespoons soy sauce	
1½	cups cubed, leftover pork	2	tablespoons toasted sesame seeds as garnish	

Method

Heat wok and add the oil. Add the vegetables and pineapple and stir fry for about 2 minutes—until the green pepper begins to go limp. Add the meat.

Combine cornstarch, sugar and seasonings; mix with chicken stock, lemon juice and soy sauce. Pour over the pork and vegetables. Cook over low heat, stirring constantly, until sauce is clear and mixture is glazed. Sprinkle with sesame seeds.

Note: Substitute chicken for pork, if you'd like.

Breaded Pork Chops

(Serves 4)

Ingredients

1	cup dry breadcrumbs	2	eggs, lightly beaten
6	tablespoons grated Parmesan cheese	1	tablespoon shortening or olive oil
	Salt and pepper	1	cup celery, diced
1	tablespoon chopped fresh parsley	2	small onions, sliced thinly
			Salt, pepper
4	loin pork chops, well trimmed Flour for dredging	½	cup Marsala, sherry or water

Method

Combine breadcrumbs, cheese, seasonings and parsley. Dredge pork chops in flour, coat with eggs and then roll them in the crumb mixture.

Heat shortening or oil in skillet, add chops and brown well on both sides. Add diced celery and sliced onions, sprinkle lightly with salt and pepper and add Marsala. Lower heat, cover pan and cook over low heat until meat is tender and well done, about 25 minutes. Serve hot.

Microwave Instructions

Follow the recipe directions, browning the chops in a ceramic casserole. Add remaining ingredients, cover and bake for 8–9 minutes per pound of pork chops on Full Power until tender. Turn the chops over partway through the cooking and rearrange them if necessary. Let stand 5–10 minutes before serving.

Pork and Vegetable Salad

(Serves 4–6)

Ingredients

1	pound lean cooked pork, cut into ½-inch cubes
1	pound green beans, blanched and halved
4	medium tomatoes, chopped
2	medium potatoes, cooked and chopped

2	zucchini, blanched and sliced
1	large green pepper, sliced
4	green onions, sliced
1	clove garlic, minced
6	pitted black olives, halved

Dressing

½	cup sour cream
¼	cup mayonnaise
2	tablespoons lemon juice
	Pinch salt and black pepper

2	teaspoons paprika
2	teaspoons Dijon mustard
2	tablespoons chopped fresh parsley

Method

Combine salad ingredients in a large salad bowl, tossing gently. Whisk dressing ingredients together until smooth. Pour dressing over salad and toss gently but thoroughly. Chill until serving.

Veal Birds Jardinière

Veal birds are thin slices of veal rolled around a ground meat mixture, browned and served with matchstick vegetables. You could use beef, chicken or turkey breasts but Chef Herbert serves these at Babsi's using veal. They're superb. (Serves 2)

Ingredients

6	2-ounce (about 60 g) scallops of veal, thinly sliced
6	teaspoons meat ends (chicken, veal or mild sausage, chopped finely or ground in a processor)
	Salt and pepper
¼	cup butter

1	shallot, finely chopped
2½	cups white wine
2½	cups chicken or veal stock
½	cup 35% cream
	Cut vegetables in season (broccoli, green beans, turnips and carrots)

Method

Flatten the veal scallops, fill with ground meat, roll them and put on a skewer. Sprinkle with salt and pepper. Sauté in butter until brown and remove them from the pan. Add the shallot, brown and deglaze with white wine, scraping all bits of meat from the pan so they become part of the gravy. Add stock and cream. Add the veal and simmer until done. Remove from pan and place on serving dish. Adjust gravy seasoning and pour over meat.

Cut vegetables into thin strips, sauté them in butter and sprinkle them over the finished birds.

Lamb M'shwi

This whole roast leg of lamb is prepared by Houria and Mustapha Zniber at their restaurant The Sultan's Tent in Toronto. The recipe comes from their native Morocco and is a favorite with regulars of the restaurant. It's served with saffron rice and is so special that lamb lovers confirm their order by phoning Mustapha a day ahead. (Serves 4)

Ingredients

1	5–7 pound (2–3 kg) leg of lamb		1	teaspoon salt
5	cloves of garlic		¼	cup butter
½	teaspoon saffron		3	cups water
¼	teaspoon freshly ground black pepper			

Method

Slice the garlic into very fine bits. Dissolve the saffron, salt and pepper in water and combine with the garlic. Remove excess surface fat from the leg of lamb and poke holes all over the surface. Spread the spice mixture over the surface of the lamb and poke it down into the prepared holes. Brush a high-sided roasting pan with oil. Place the lamb in the pan and dot with butter. Place in a 450°F oven for 20 minutes, turning the roast over several times. Reduce the heat to 400°F and pour 3 cups of water into the pan. Cook for 2 hours, turning once halfway through the cooking time. Add extra water, if needed. Test lamb with a meat thermometer (170°F). Remove lamb from water. Place on a rack in a roaster and leave at 350°F until crisp, about 30 minutes.

Noisettes of Lamb with Basil Cream Sauce

This is an elegant entrée featured at The Four Season's Hotel—Yorkville, in Toronto. It uses the simplest of cooking methods—a reduction of pan juices and wine with cream which then is poured over rare lamb sirloin. Fresh lamb is wonderful when it is in season, but I have often done this with frozen lamb when it is at the market for a special price. Chef Niels Kjeldson's technique guarantees exquisite taste and flavor. (Serves 4)

Ingredients

12	1½-ounce lamb noisettes—cut from the loin	2	teaspoons fresh basil
	Salt, pepper	½	cup cream
1½	tablespoons butter		Carrots, turnip, celery root, green beans, cut into thin slivers
2	teaspoons shallots, chopped		
¼	cup white wine		

Method

Season the noisettes with salt and pepper and sauté in the butter until pink in the centre (2 minutes each side, approximately). Remove and keep warm. Discard the excess fat, add the shallots and sweat for a minute, then deglaze pan with white wine, reduce by half, add the basil and the cream. Simmer 1 minute.

Ladle the sauce onto a hot dinner plate and arrange the lamb noisettes on top. Garnish with the vegetable batonettes which have been cooked in boiling salted water until crisp (about 5 minutes).

POULTRY

Poulet Basquaise 51

Curried Chicken with Shrimp 48

Chicken Curry O'Neill 49

Chicken in Crystal Fold 50

Chicken in a Clay Baker 52

Chicken Pot Pie 53

Canneloni Stuffed with Chicken 54

Turkey or Chicken Strata 55

Turkey Terrine 56

Roasted Cornish Hen (Kamama) 58

Rabbit with Honey and Tomato Sauce 58

Roast Duck with Normandy Sauce 60

Curried Chicken with Shrimp

CP Air Steward Alex Schur prepared this elegant dinner for two for us last year. I like to double it and invite the neighbors. (Serves 2)

Ingredients

2	chicken breast halves, boned, skinned and cut into serving pieces	1	tablespoon curry powder, mild Madras
2–3	tablespoons flour	6	medium-sized fresh shrimp, cleaned and deveined
	Pinch of salt and freshly ground black pepper	¼	cup chicken stock
2	tablespoons light vegetable oil	¼	cup 35% cream
1	onion, finely chopped	½	pound (250 g) long grain rice
1	clove garlic, finely chopped	2	tablespoons butter

Garnish

1	banana, peeled and sliced	1	tablespoon almonds, sliced and toasted
2	peaches, halved, drained and sliced	1	tablespoon parsley, chopped
4	maraschino cherries		

Method

Coat chicken pieces with mixture of flour, salt and pepper, shaking to remove excess. Heat oil, add chicken pieces and sauté until golden brown. Add chopped onion and garlic and sauté until transparent. Sprinkle with curry powder, add shrimp and cook until tender. Add chicken stock and cream and bring to the boil, stirring from time to time. Taste and adjust seasoning, if necessary. Remove to a hot platter and keep warm. Prepare rice following instructions on the package. Melt butter in a sauté pan and toss in sliced fruit turning until glazed.

Arrange rice ring on serving platter and place the curried chicken in the centre. Garnish around the sides with the glazed banana, peaches, and cherries. Sprinkle with slivered almonds and chopped parsley.

Chicken Curry O'Neill

Sandra O'Neill tells us that curry is the spaghetti sauce of India and she should know. She was raised there. Her mother became an authority on Indian cuisine, watching the cook prepare the many different dishes that made up their evening meal. Now, Sandra cooks only during the brief times when she is not on stage at her own dinner theatre in Toronto— O'Neill's. (Serves 6)

Ingredients

3	tablespoons vegetable oil	1	heaping teaspoon ground coriander
3	medium onions, diced		
7	cloves garlic, very finely chopped	1	4½-pound (2 kg) chicken, cut into 8 pieces
1	slice of ginger, about 1 inch thick, finely chopped		Salt
1	heaping tablespoon tumeric	¼	package creamed coconut— available at Indian grocery stores
1	heaping tablespoon paprika		
2	large tomatoes, diced	1	lemon, juiced

Method

Heat oil in a large frying pan and add onions. Sauté until golden and remove half to a bowl. Add garlic and ginger to the remaining onions and continue to cook for another 5 minutes. Add tumeric and paprika, stirring with a wooden spoon for a few minutes. Add tomatoes and allow to cook for 2 minutes. Add coriander. Remove the pan from the stove and add the chicken. Blend together well. Return to stove and sauté for about 10 minutes, stirring occasionally. Add water to cover and simmer for ½ hour. The chicken will be pink and firm. Add reserved onions. Taste and add salt or other seasonings, if necessary.

About 5 minutes before serving, add coconut and stir. Then add lemon juice. Taste again. Serve with yogurt salad.

Microwave Instructions

In a large ceramic casserole (the type that may be used on top of the stove and in the microwave), follow recipe directions on top of the stove, until you add the chicken; sauté as directed for 10 minutes. Add a ½ cup of water, cover and microwave 7-8 minutes per pound of chicken on Full Power, rearranging and turning chicken pieces over halfway through the cooking. The chicken should be tender and the juices run clear when pierced. Add remaining ingredients and let stand, covered, 5-10 minutes before serving.

Chicken in Crystal Fold

This is Lucy Waverman's French-Chinese adaptation, which can be prepared ahead of time. It is a delightful main course, using French technique and Chinese ingredients. (Makes 6–8 servings)

Ingredients

1	medium–large eggplant		Salt and pepper
6	Chinese dried mushrooms	2	heads iceberg lettuce
1	cup water chestnuts	8	6–8 ounce chicken breasts
1½	tablespoons vegetable oil		(200 g) each, boned
1	cup finely chopped onion	1½	tablespoons vegetable oil
1	tablespoon soy sauce	1½	tablespoons butter

Sauce

¼	cup dry white wine	¼	teaspoon Chinese chili sauce
2	cups chicken stock		(optional)*
1	small ripe papaya		Salt and pepper
½	tablespoon hoisin sauce*		

Method

Place eggplant on a cookie sheet and bake at 350°F for 45 minutes or until soft; let cool. Split open and remove pulp, squeezing out liquid and removing as many seeds as possible. Chop pulp and reserve. Discard skins.

Soak mushrooms in warm water for 15 minutes or until soft. Remove stalk and dice finely. Chop water chestnuts finely.

In a large frying pan, heat oil until hot. Sauté onion until limp, add mushrooms and water chestnuts; stir together. Add reserved eggplant and combine. Remove from heat. Season with soy sauce, salt and pepper. The mixture should be highly seasoned. Cool.

Remove core from lettuces. Gently take off leaves; try to keep them whole. You will need approximately 16 leaves.

Bring a large pot of water to a boil. Throw in lettuce leaves and boil for 1 minute. Drain and refresh leaves under cold running water.

Cover chicken breasts with plastic wrap or waxed paper. Using the back of a cleaver or bottom of a large pot, flatten breasts slightly. Season with salt and pepper.

Spread out lettuce leaves. Put ½ heaped tablespoon of eggplant mixture on lettuce. Place a chicken breast on top. Cover with more

*Note: Hoisin sauce and Chinese chili sauce are available at Chinese food stores.

eggplant. Fold lettuce leaf over. Cover with another leaf to make a lettuce-leaf package. Tuck in ends. Loop a piece of string a couple of times around package and tie.

In a large frying pan, melt oil and butter over high heat. Quickly brown packages on each side, a few at a time; set aside. The dish can be made ahead to this point.

Sauce

In the same pan, over high heat, pour in wine and reduce until syrupy. Pour in chicken stock and boil down until 1 cup is left.

Purée papaya in a food processor or blender or mash by hand. Stir into sauce. Stir in hoisin sauce. Taste for seasoning. If you like a spicy flavor, add chili sauce. Bring to a boil again. This can be prepared ahead of time and reheated.

Place chicken packages on a rack over a cookie sheet and bake at 375°F for 20-30 minutes, depending on their thickness. Serve with the sauce.

Poulet Basquaise

When Maison Basque chef Roger Dufau arrives on the set, there is a sense of excitement. People seem to gravitate to Studio Seven for a look at the handsome chef at work and a taste of whatever he is preparing. This typical Basque country dish was a particular favorite. (Serves 4)

Ingredients

4	tablespoons olive or vegetable oil		1	tablespoon parsley, finely chopped
1	4½ pound (2 kg) chicken, cut into 8 serving pieces			Sprinkling of thyme (optional)
			1	cup dry white wine
1	Spanish onion, chopped		1	can (540 mL) tomatoes
2	green peppers, seeded and sliced		1	slice Parma or Bayonne ham, chopped
2	cloves garlic, finely chopped			Salt and pepper

Method

Heat oil in heavy casserole and sauté chicken pieces until golden brown. Remove and keep warm. Sauté chopped onion, green peppers and garlic in the oil until tender. After 2 minutes add the parsley and thyme. Return chicken pieces to casserole, add dry white wine, and cook over high heat until wine is reduced to half the original quantity—about 5 minutes. Add tomatoes and ham. Season with salt and pepper. Cover casserole and let the chicken simmer for 25 minutes or until tender. Serve with rice or Gratin Dauphinois (p. 89).

Chicken in a Clay Baker

A porous, unglazed clay pot is perfect for a complete meal-in-a-dish. There's no precooking. Everything is added to the pot and allowed to bake. The water evaporates and the food sizzles happily, combining flavors exquisitely. Irena Chalmers brought this idea as a sample of the recipes in her small book *Clay Cookery*. (Serves 4)

Ingredients

½	pound (250 g) bacon, diced	1	square unsweetened chocolate, cut into pieces
2	3¼-pound (1.5 kg) chickens, cut in half lengthwise	1	teaspoon dried thyme
3	tablespoons flour		Salt and pepper
2	medium-sized onions, finely chopped	1	can (213 mL) plum tomatoes
2	cloves garlic, finely chopped	1½	cups whole small mushrooms
2	carrots, finely chopped	3	tablespoons butter
3	stalks celery, finely chopped	1	can (284 mL) water chestnuts
2	cups chicken broth	3	tablespoons finely chopped parsley
1	cup red wine		

Method

Soak a 4-quart clay baker in cold water for 15 minutes. Fry the bacon until crisp. Drain on paper towels and leave to one side. Dredge the chicken in flour and place it in the clay baker with the onions, garlic, carrots and celery. Add the chicken broth and wine. Stir in the chocolate and thyme. Season with salt and pepper. Add the tomatoes with the juice from the can. Add the crisp bacon. Cover and place in a cold oven. Set the temperature at 400°F and cook 1 hour. In the meantime, fry the mushrooms in hot butter until lightly browned. Remove the cover and add the mushrooms and water chestnuts to the chicken. Continue cooking, uncovered, for 10 minutes. Garnish with parsley.

Microwave Instructions

Layer bacon on paper towels. Cover. Microwave at Full Power 7–8 minutes. Proceed as directed but omit salt until the end of the cooking and reduce the chicken broth to 1 cup. Microwave, covered, at Full Power 25 minutes. Turn chicken over. Microwave again, covered, at Full Power 15–20 minutes until chickens are tender. Add mushrooms and water chestnuts; microwave, uncovered, 2–3 minutes.

Chicken Pot Pie

A traditional chicken pot pie is made with flaky pastry but we think that this quick biscuit version is just as special. When making the biscuits, let the dough rest for a few minutes on the board and then either roll as you would roll pastry to cover the top completely or use cookie cutters and pop the small, round biscuits on top. Either way is simple and delicious. (Serves 6)

Ingredients

2	cups cooked chicken	1	cup frozen peas
2	cups chicken stock	2	tablespoons butter
1/2	teaspoon salt	1	medium onion, chopped
1/4	teaspoon pepper	1	cup mushrooms, sliced
1/2	teaspoon thyme leaves	4	tablespoons butter, at room temperature
1/2	teaspoon chervil		
4	potatoes, peeled and cubed	4	tablespoons flour
4	carrots, peeled and sliced		

Topping

1	cup all-purpose flour	2	tablespoons shortening
2	teaspoons baking powder	1/2	cup milk
1/2	teaspoon salt		

Method

Place cooked chicken in casserole. Combine chicken stock, salt and pepper, thyme and chervil in large saucepan. Bring to the boil. Add potatoes and simmer covered for 10 minutes. Add carrots and simmer 10 minutes more. Stir in peas. With slotted spoon, remove vegetables to casserole with chicken. Reserve stock. Sauté onion and mushrooms in butter for 5-7 minutes. Add to chicken and vegetable mixture in casserole.

To thicken stock blend the 4 tablespoons butter with the 4 tablespoons flour in a bowl. Add to heated stock, a small bit at a time, until stock is desired thickness. Pour thickened stock over vegetable mixture.

Topping

Combine flour, baking powder and salt. Cut in shortening until the mixture resembles coarse meal. Add milk, all at once and stir to moisten dry ingredients. Turn out onto lightly floured surface. Knead about 20 times. Roll dough to fit top of casserole. If you prefer less crust, cut rounds with a floured cookie cutter and place these on top. Lay on top of casserole dish, sealing edges. Cut slits in dough to allow steam to escape. Bake at 425°F for 15 minutes or until top is golden. Reduce heat to 300°F. Continue baking until pie is heated through—about 20 minutes if the chicken mixture is warm, longer if it has been allowed to cool. When the gravy bubbles through the slits in the pastry, the pie is ready.

Canneloni Stuffed with Chicken

The talented fingers of Holt Renfrew's Dacia Moss whipped this delicious dish together for us. It may be prepared in advance and even frozen before baking. We substituted spinach pasta once and loved the result. (Serves 4)

Ingredients

½ pound (225 g) fresh pasta cut into 3-inch squares *or*

12 packaged dry canneloni noodles

Filling

2 deboned chicken breast halves, marinated in ¼ cup lemon juice
¼ cup butter
1 egg, lightly beaten
1 cup Ricotta cheese

3 tablespoons grated Romano cheese
½ cup slivered almonds
3 tablespoons fresh parsley, chopped
Salt and pepper to taste

Sauce

¼ cup butter
2 tablespoons finely chopped onion
¼ cup all-purpose flour

1 cup chicken stock
½ cup heavy cream
2 tablespoons dry vermouth
Salt and pepper to taste

Method

Boil pasta in 4 quarts of salted water to which 2 tablespoons olive oil have been added. Cook 6 minutes or until firm but tender, *al dente*. Plunge into cold water. If using dry canneloni, prepare according to package directions.

To prepare filling, sauté chicken in butter until tender and cooked through. Chop into medium-sized pieces. Add egg, cheeses, almonds, parsley, salt and pepper. Set aside.

The sauce is made by adding ¼ cup butter to pan juices from cooked chicken. Add chopped onion to butter and cook until soft. Add flour and cook 2 minutes. Stir in chicken stock and when thick and smooth add cream, vermouth, salt and pepper.

Cover the bottom of a baking pan with a little sauce. Remove fresh pasta from cold water and dry each sheet with a paper towel. Place 2–3 tablespoons of filling on each sheet and roll into a tube, or fill each cooked canneloni. Place in baking pan taking care not to pack them too tightly together. Cover with remaining sauce. Top with a little extra Romano or Parmesan cheese. Bake in a preheated 375°F oven for 25 minutes or until lightly brown and heated through.

Microwave Instructions

Arrange as directed in a glass baking dish. Bake, uncovered, 4 minutes on Full Power. Rotate the dish if necessary and bake 8–10 minutes on Medium (50% Power) until heated through.

Turkey or Chicken Strata

If there is bread, eggs and milk in the house on the day after a turkey dinner, make this simple, splendid casserole. Just make it well enough in advance for the bread to absorb fully the egg and milk mixture. (Serves 6)

Ingredients

1	loaf French bread, cut into ½-inch slices, crusts removed
1½	cups turkey or chicken, cooked and chopped
½	pound (250 g) sharp Cheddar cheese, shredded (2 cups)
½	green pepper, chopped

1	small onion, chopped
6	eggs
2	cups milk
½	teaspoon curry powder
¼	teaspoon dry mustard
	Salt and freshly ground pepper to taste

Method

Lightly grease a 12 × 8 inch baking dish. Line with enough bread slices to cover bottom. Combine turkey or chicken, 1½ cups cheese, green pepper and onion. Spread over bread layer. Top with enough additional bread slices to cover turkey layer. Combine eggs, milk and seasonings. Pour over mixture. Sprinkle with remaining cheese. Cover and chill several hours or overnight. Bake, uncovered in preheated 325°F oven until golden brown, about 45 minutes. Garnish with parsley sprigs.

Turkey Terrine

This terrine serves a double purpose. It makes a wonderful cold loaf for a summer lunch party and sandwich filling for a picnic. I make it on a weekend morning in the heat of summer and it fills out the week admirably—first for guests, then for supper sandwiches and as an addition to a salad-bowl meal. If you find the prospect of making turkey broth too daunting, use canned consommé or chicken broth. (Serves 8–10)

Turkey Broth

(Makes about 3 cups)

Ingredients

2½ pounds (1 kg) turkey thighs, approximately two	1 stalk celery with leaves, cut into 1-inch pieces
1 carrot, peeled and cut into 1-inch pieces	1 medium onion, quartered
	4 cups water

Method

Skin and bone the thighs. Discard the skins and reserve the bones. Weigh out 15 ounces (425 g) of meat for the turkey terrine and refrigerate until ready to make it.

With a cleaver, crack the thigh bones in two places. In a 2½-quart saucepan, combine the bones, remaining meat and scraps with the carrot, celery and onion. Add enough water to cover, about 4 cups. Bring to a boil over moderate heat, skimming off any scum that rises to the top. Reduce the heat to low, cover and simmer for 2½ hours. Let broth cool to room temperature. Freeze 1½ cups of broth until mushy and use for making the terrine. You will have 1–1½ cups broth left if you want hot turkey sandwiches.

Ingredients

½ cup plus 1 tablespoon dry skim milk	1 piece of onion, walnut-size, cut in half
2 teaspoons salt	15 ounces (about 400–500 g) turkey meat, cut into 1-inch pieces
1 teaspoon white pepper	
¼ teaspoon 5-spice powder (available at Oriental grocery stores (see p. 146 for home-made version)	5 ounces (about 100–200 g) turkey fat, cut into 1-inch pieces
2 teaspoons cinnamon	5 pounds (2 kg) ice, about 4 standard trays
1½ cups turkey broth, frozen in an ice cubes tray until just mushy	Black olives
	Red or green pepper

Method

Preheat oven to 250°F. In a small bowl, mix ½ cup dry milk, salt, pepper and spices. Divide equally between 2 dishes and set aside. Divide the half-frozen broth equally between two cups.

In a food processor, using the steel blade, process one of the onion pieces, half the turkey, half the turkey fat, and half the spice mixture until smooth, scraping down the side of the bowl as necessary.

With the machine on, spoon the mushy frozen turkey broth from one of the two cups through the feed tube, a tablespoon at a time, waiting about 3 seconds between spoonfuls. After adding half of the first cup of the broth, scrape down the side of the bowl. Turn the machine on again and add the remaining half of first cup of broth gradually through the feed tube. Let the machine run for 60 seconds, stopping twice to scrape down the side and around the bottom of the bowl. The meat mixture should be fluffy and smooth. Empty into a bowl, cover with plastic wrap and set aside.

Make a second batch the same way, using the remaining onion, turkey, turkey fat, spices and frozen broth. Then return the first batch to the machine and process the two together for 15 seconds to blend, scraping the sides of the bowl.

Butter a 4-cup loaf pan. Pack the meat mixture carefully into it, spreading it carefully to avoid air pockets. For a touch of color, black olives or blanched strips of red or green pepper may be added to the terrine as you layer the mixture into the pan. They should be dusted with flour first to hold them in place for neater slicing.

Mound the mixture slightly in the middle. Smooth the top with a spatula or spreader and if you wish, make a few diagonal slashes for decoration. Tap firmly on counter to settle.

Dissolve the remaining 1 tablespoon dry milk in 2 tablespoons water. Place the terrine in the centre of the preheated oven. Bake until the internal temperature reaches 155°F–158°F. This usually takes about 1 hour and 45 minutes. After 45 minutes, brush the top of the terrine generously with the milk.

Place the ice in a large pan in your sink. Fill with cold water to a depth of 3 inches. As soon as the terrine comes out of the oven, place it in the ice water. Make sure no water splashes onto the meat. Let the terrine cool in the water until the internal temperature drops to 125°F or less. *Note:* You can skip this step and place the terrine directly in your refrigerator to cool. The texture may be somewhat less compact, but the taste will be the same.

Remove the terrine from the pan and pat dry with a paper towel. Refrigerate in a plastic food storage bag. The terrine may be sliced after 2 hours of refrigeration, but the flavor improves after 2 days.

Roasted Cornish Hen (Kamama)

Moroccan feasting begins with luscious lamb soup and ends with rich sweet desserts or ice cream. While many of us think that Moroccan cuisine is Couscous only, adventurous diners have tried other succulent entrées—like this one, prepared in Montreal by Hafid Zniber at the Menara restaurant. Serve it with a diced cucumber salad. (Serves 2)

Ingredients

1	Cornish hen		1	teaspoon cinnamon
3	onions, sliced thickly		1/4	teaspoon saffron
1/4	cup seedless raisins		1/4	cup vegetable oil
1	teaspoon salt		1	cup water
1/2	teaspoon pepper			

Method

Mix all ingredients together, except the hen and water, and place in a saucepan large enough to hold the bird. Turn heat to low and add the hen. Turn to coat completely with the spices and onion mixture. Add 1 cup water, cover and simmer for 1/2 hour or until the onions are cooked. Remove the hen and place it in a pan in the oven at 350°F. Leave until brown, about 15 minutes. Meanwhile, continue cooking the sauce until it reduces to half. Serve the hen and top with the sauce.

Rabbit with Honey and Tomato Sauce

Dinner at the Sultan's Tent restaurant in Toronto or at the Menara restaurant in Montreal means a full-course traditional Moroccan meal— from soup (harira) to sweets (grioosh). This recipe is one of our favorites, known as m'rouzia which needs only a side salad of tomato and green pepper with cumin sauce to satisfy. The sauce bakes onto the rabbit, while the tomato cooks down to a thickness which is a mere whisper of a garnish. Delicious (Serves 3-4)

Ingredients

1	3-5 pound (1.5-2 kg) rabbit		1/2	teaspoon salt
2	onions, finely chopped		1/4	teaspoon saffron
1	tablespoon cinnamon		1/4	cup water
1/4	teaspoon nutmeg		1/4	cup butter or margarine
1	teaspoon ginger			Water
1	teaspoon or less of freshly ground black pepper		3/4	cup liquid honey

Tomato Sauce

1 can (284 mL) tomatoes	1 tablespoon cinnamon
Pinch gum arabic (optional)	3 tablespoons honey
Few drops orange blossom water (optional)	

Garnish
Handful of browned, blanched almonds

Method

Wash the rabbit and dry with paper towels. Cut into 6–8 pieces. Leave the legs whole. Place the onions in a sauté pan and measure and dissolve the spices in $\frac{1}{4}$ cup water. Add the spice mixture to the onions. Place the rabbit pieces in the spice-onion mixture and turn and coat the meat completely. Add the butter or margarine. Turn the heat on at low and allow the meat to simmer for about 8–10 minutes or until everything is well mixed. Cover the rabbit with water, cover the pot and continue cooking until the rabbit is tender—about 1–1½ hours. Uncover and add the honey. Continue cooking, without the lid, until the mixture is reduced. It will be thick and shiny. Carefully lift the rabbit from the sauce and place it in a low pan in a 450°F oven for a few minutes or until the rabbit is golden brown and crisp. Meanwhile, continue to reduce the sauce.

Tomato Sauce
To prepare the tomato sauce drain the tomatoes through a sieve, pushing all of the liquid and seeds through. Place the pulp in a saucepan with the optional ingredients and cinnamon and allow it to cook and reduce until thick. All the liquid should be gone. Make sure that you stir often and scrape the bottom with a wooden spoon so the sauce doesn't burn. Add 3 tablespoons of honey and continue to cook. It will be thick and brown and resemble jam.

Place the rabbit on the plate. Pour the reduced sauce over top, add the tomato sauce in dabs and sprinkle with the browned almonds.

Roast Duck with Normandy Sauce

A juicy, succulent duck with crisp golden brown skin is still a real treat and the freshness of the sauce is a good contrast to the richness of the duck. This recipe combines two cooking methods. Steaming gives a better flavor and tender juicy meat while roasting adds crispness and makes the duck easier to carve. (Serves 4)

Ingredients

1   5–6 pound (2.5 kg) duck
1   cup chicken broth, stock or
     water

Normandy Sauce

3   tablespoons brown sugar
1   tablespoon cornstarch
     Pinch salt
¼   teaspoon freshly grated
     nutmeg
     Pinch ground cloves

1   cup apple juice
2   tablespoons apple brandy
     (Calvados)
2   tablespoons butter
     Apple or crabapple slices for
     garnish

Method

Steaming
Prick duck skin all over. Put steamer or rack in large, deep pot and add broth, stock or water. Set duck, breast side up on steamer. Bring liquid to a simmer, then cover and steam duck gently for 1 hour. Meanwhile, prepare Normandy Sauce. At the end of the hour, remove duck and carefully pat dry.

Roasting
Place one rack in the middle of the oven and a second rack in lower third position. Preheat oven to 425°F. Prick duck all over once more to release fat and brush with Normandy Sauce. Set duck on a wire cake rack or directly on the oven rack, place large drip pan on bottom rack. Roast duck for 20 minutes then lower heat to 350°F, baste with additional sauce and roast another 20–30 minutes. To test if bird is done, pierce the fattest part of the thigh with a skewer; if the juices have a pinkish cast, the meat is rare, if the juices run clear, the meat is well done. Remove from oven and let rest 10 minutes before carving. Garnish platter with apple slices and sauce. Pass remaining sauce with duck.

Normandy Sauce

In a small saucepan stir together the brown sugar, cornstarch, salt, nutmeg and cloves. Add apple juice and stir over medium heat until the mixture starts to boil. Add brandy. Remove from heat and stir in the butter.

If using a microwave, combine brown sugar, cornstarch, salt, nutmeg, cloves and apple juice in a 4-cup glass measure. Cook on full power for 2–3 minutes, stirring occasionally until mixture starts to boil. Add brandy and stir in the butter.

FISH

Fisherman's Chowder in Crust   64

Sole with Apple   67

Fish in Parchment   63

Salmon in Puff Pastry with Sorrel Sauce   66

Creole Fish with Rice   68

Baked Mackerel   65

Baked Fish with Broccoli and Mussels   70

Mussels in Black Bean Sauce   69

Shrimp with Lemon and Ginger   71

Sauté of Shrimp with Wild Rice, Mushrooms and Tomato   72

Spaghetti Alla Puttanesca   73

Fish in Parchment

This traditional method for steaming fish, with or without vegetables is modern in every respect. It enhances the flavor, while reducing the calories. Cook the fish with vegetables for a main course or garnish with herbs for an appetizer. The parchment paper will puff up, so serve immediately. (Serves 4)

Ingredients

2	tablespoons shallots or scallions, minced	4	ounces (125 g) baby carrots, blanched and chilled, about 4–6 small carrots
4	fish fillets (salmon, red snapper, cod, halibut)	½	cup dry white wine
1	pound (500 g) assorted vegetables (cherry tomatoes, whole button mushrooms, zucchini, summer squash) sliced	2	tablespoons butter
			Salt and pepper
			Basil, tarragon or dill sprigs
4	ounces (125 g) asparagus tips or broccoli spears, about 8 spears		Olive oil
			Lemon slices and parsley sprigs for garnish

Method

For each person you will need a large piece of parchment or foil, approximately 9 inches by 12 inches. Fold paper in half and butter the bottom half. Place equal quantities of shallots or scallions on it covered by a fish fillet. Surround this with the vegetables. Sprinkle with the wine, dot with butter and season with salt and pepper. Lay the herb sprigs on top. Fold over the paper and cut so that there is a 1-inch margin around the fish and vegetables. Crimp the edges of the paper to prevent air holes. Brush the top of the paper with olive oil. Refrigerate on a baking sheet, if prepared in advance.

Preheat oven to 450°F. Bake fish for 10–15 minutes or until the fish goes from translucent to opaque. Arrange on individual plates; slit edges of paper packets, roll back slightly and garnish with lemon slices and parsley sprigs. Serve immediately.

Fisherman's Chowder in Crust

Bruno Marti demonstrated this recipe using whipping cream and other high calorie ingredients. We changed it to cut calories and found this delightful result. I always have a supply of chowder in the freezer for unexpected parties. Often when shrimp, salmon and scallops are too expensive, I'll substitute other lower-priced fish such as perch, turbot or cod. As long as there is slightly more than 1½ pounds (700 g) of mixed fish, the chowder is delicious.

Because we have substituted for the whipping cream, the sauce may separate. For a smoother and richer sauce, use 35% cream in place of the milk. (Serves 6)

Ingredients

1	cup broccoli, 2 stalks, cut into small pieces	½	pound (about 250 g) sole
2	carrots, thinly sliced	1½	cups dry white wine
¼	cup butter or vegetable oil	1	14-ounce can (385 mL) evaporated milk
5	medium shallots, peeled and chopped	6	mushrooms, sliced
¼	pound (125 g) scallops (about 4 medium-sized ones)		Salt and freshly ground white pepper
½	pound (about 250 g) shrimp (4 large)	1	16-ounce (454 g) package puff pastry
¼	pound (about 125 g) salmon (the tail is best—no waste)	1	egg yolk mixed with 1 table-spoon water for wash

You'll need 6 individual ovenproof soup dishes. If these do not come to hand, there are aluminum foil pans in the supermarkets which work quite well.

Method

Steam the carrots and broccoli for 5 minutes and chill immediately in ice water.

Cut the scallops in quarters, the shrimp in thirds and the rest of the fish into bite-sized pieces. If there is skin on the salmon, remove it. Heat the butter or oil in a medium saucepan over moderate heat and add the shallots and fish. Stir and sauté for 3 minutes or until the fish has lost its shine. Add the wine and stir to remove any bits that may be sticking to the bottom of the pan. Strain liquid through a sieve and reserve.

Return the wine to the pan, add milk and, over moderate heat, bring to the boil. Allow much of the liquid to evaporate. Add salt and pepper and taste to correct the seasoning. Divide the fish between the 6 dishes and lay mushrooms, carrots and broccoli over top. Ladle the broth over top and set aside while you roll the crust. Preheat the oven to 425°F. Divide the puff pastry into 6. Roll each to a round which will overlap the dish by about ¾ inch. Brush the pastry with egg wash around the outside edge, about ¾ inch into the centre. Turn upside down. Wrap this pastry over the top and down the side of the dish to hug it. Brush the entire top surface with egg wash. Repeat until all 6 are done. Keep them cool before baking. Do not prick the pastry as it puffs up beautifully. A hole in the centre would deflate this. Bake for 20 minutes or until the crust is high and nicely browned. Leave out for 10 minutes before serving. They are very hot.

Note: If you wish to prepare in advance, roll the crust, brush with egg and refrigerate until baking time. Then place pastry on top of each dish.

Baked Mackerel

Poaching the fish for a few minutes before baking in a tomato sauce makes this fish dish different and delicious. We like it with mashed potatoes. (Serves 6)

Ingredients

2	pounds (1 kg) mackerel steaks	⅓	cup dry vermouth
¼	teaspoon pepper	1	teaspoon garlic, crushed
1	teaspoon salt	½	cup soft breadcrumbs
1½	cups tomatoes, diced	2	tablespoons butter
1	cup mushrooms, sliced		

Method

Heat oven to 350°F. Rinse and dry fish. Sprinkle with salt and pepper. Poach fish in water to cover for 2–3 minutes, turning once. Place in shallow baking dish. Combine tomatoes, mushrooms, vermouth and garlic in saucepan; bring to a boil. Pour hot sauce over fish. Mix crumbs and melted butter, sprinkle on top. Bake for 20 minutes or until crumbs are brown and fish flakes.

Microwave Instructions

Place steaks evenly in a large, glass baking dish with no overlapping pieces. Sprinkle with salt and pepper. Combine tomatoes, mushrooms, vermouth and garlic in a 4-cup glass measure. Cook 3–5 minutes on Full Power, until the sauce boils. Pour over the fish. Mix crumbs and butter and sprinkle over the fish. Bake, covered, 8–10 minutes on Full Power, rearranging and turning steaks if necessary partway through the cooking until the fish flakes.

Salmon in Puff Pastry with Sorrel Sauce

These delicious and unusual salmon "fishes" would be ideal for a special dinner and create lively conversation at the table. Well worth the little extra care needed, this dish appeals to the eye as well as the taste buds. Try serving them with asparagus, broccoli or summer squash. (Serves 4)

Ingredients

Filling

1	pound (500 g) leeks	1	egg
4	tablespoons butter	1	tablespoon cream
	Salt and pepper to taste		Salt
1	pound (500 g) puff pastry		
4	fillets of salmon (halibut, cod or bass)		

Method

First prepare the filling. Trim and wash the leeks. Use the white and pale green parts only. Cut into julienne strips and cook gently in the butter for about 20 minutes, until soft. Season with salt and pepper.

Preheat oven to 375°F. Roll out the puff pastry. With a sharp knife and a stencil, cut out 8 fish shapes. Place 4 of these on a baking sheet. Divide the leeks into 4 portions and spoon on to the pastry bases. Cover with the salmon. With a brush dipped in water, wet the rim of the pastry base and place another fish outline over the top of the fish and leeks. Press edges together firmly. Decorate pastry tops with scraps of dough. Beat the egg, add the cream and a pinch of salt. Brush the pastry fish with the egg glaze. Using the sharp end of a knife, seal by just drawing the tip through the pastry at ¼-inch intervals to seal but not to cut the pastry. If the pastry has become too soft, chill in the refrigerator and repaint with the glaze. Bake in the oven for 25–35 minutes until golden brown.

Sorrel Sauce

Ingredients

2	tablespoons butter	2	cups good fish stock or mock fish stock (see below)
½	cup shallots, minced		
1	cup fresh sorrel, finely chopped	½	cup heavy cream
		1	tablespoon arrowroot
			Salt and pepper to taste

Method

Place the butter in a saucepan, add the shallots and cook until soft. Add the sorrel and cook over medium heat for 3–4 minutes. Add fish stock or mock fish stock (see below) and bring to the boil, reducing by half. Stir in the cream mixed with the arrowroot and boil for another 5 minutes. Season with salt and pepper to taste.

Note: If sorrel is unavailable, fresh spinach with a splash of white wine vinegar can be used.

Mock Fish Stock

(Makes 2 cups stock)

Ingredients

1	8-ounce (227 mL) bottle clam juice	Carrot
½	cup dry white wine	Onion
½	cup water	Celery
		Parsley

Method

Bring this all to the boiling point, reduce the heat and simmer for 30 minutes. Discard the vegetables.

Sole with Apple

Sometimes the simplest things are the best. (Serves 4)

Ingredients

1	pound (500 g) sole or other white fish fillets, thawed, if frozen	3		tablespoons butter
		1		large apple
2	tablespoons flour	½		cup plain yogurt
	Salt and pepper	¼–½		teaspoon curry powder

Method

Lightly coat the fillets in a mixture of flour, salt and pepper, shaking off any excess. Melt the butter in a large frypan and sauté the fillets until golden on both sides, turning once. This will take about 5 minutes.

Meanwhile, core the apple and cut into wedges, keeping skin on for color. Remove sole to warm platter and keep warm. Add apple slices, yogurt, curry and a pinch of salt and pepper to pan. Cook, uncovered over medium heat until apples are softened, about 3–5 minutes, stirring often. Pour over the fish and serve.

Creole Fish with Rice

Cod or haddock may be used to replace Boston bluefish in this top-of-the-stove supper. Low in calories and cost, high in nutritional value and taste, this dish can be made with frozen fish.

If you buy frozen fish choose a package that has no frost visible on the package and no feel of frost when pressed firmly. Frost-free packages assure that the fish was fast frozen recently enough for the quality to be tops. (Serves 2–4)

Ingredients

1	pound (500 g) Boston bluefish fillets	1	can (540 mL) tomatoes
1	cup onion, sliced	½	cup green pepper, chopped
1	cup celery, sliced	1	teaspoon garlic
2	tablespoons margarine or cooking oil	½	teaspoon chili powder
1	tablespoon flour		Dash of pepper
		4	cups hot cooked rice

Method

Cut fish into 1½-inch pieces. Cook onion and celery in margarine or oil in saucepan until onion is tender but not brown. Stir in flour. Add tomatoes, green pepper and seasonings; mix well. Cover and simmer about 20 minutes. Add fish, simmer uncovered about 10 minutes or until fish flakes easily with fork. Serve over rice.

Microwave Instructions

In a 2-quart glass casserole combine the onion, celery and margarine. Cook, uncovered, 2–4 minutes on Full Power until softened. Stir in flour. Add tomatoes, green pepper and seasonings and mix well. Cover and cook for 4–6 minutes on Full Power. Add fish, cover, and cook for 4–5 minutes on Full Power, or until the fish flakes with a fork. Stir once partway through the cooking.

Mussels in Black Bean Sauce

Michael Vaughan, The Mussel Man, with his shop in downtown Toronto, sells mollusks of all kinds, but specializes in cultivated mussels. He brought them along to Studio Seven and dispensed wisdom about mussels to the delight of everyone. Here are some of his hints:

• To test for freshness, move the shell sideways; if it shifts, throw it out.

• Only use fresh mussels and store them in the refrigerator (if you must) covered with a damp cloth, never with water. They will keep for a week.

• Open mussels are not necessarily dead mussels. To test, drop each open mussel into a bowl of water and push it with your hands. If it still doesn't close, then discard it.

• When cooking mussels, allow 1½ pounds (about 700 g) per person.

• The best and simplest way to prepare them is to steam them over boiling water or sauté them in oil.

Here's Michael's favorite recipe. (Serves 2)

Ingredients

1	tablespoon vegetable oil	2	ounces dry sherry
2	tablespoons butter		Salt and pepper
1	small onion, chopped	3	pounds (1½ kg) fresh mussels
3	cloves garlic		
1 or 2	tablespoons black bean sauce (available in Chinese grocery stores)		

Method

Rinse mussels and remove the hairs and anything that is attached. Pour the oil into a wok and heat. Add the butter. Add onion and garlic and sauté for 1 or 2 minutes. Add 1 tablespoon of the black bean sauce, the sherry, salt, pepper and mussels. Stir-fry for 5–10 minutes or until all of the mussels are open. Taste and check for seasoning. If you wish, add more black bean sauce. Serve immediately.

Baked Fish with Broccoli and Mussels

This fish casserole forms the basis for a company meal of consommé, pumpernickel toasts, tossed mushroom salad, papaya, and chocolate truffles with coffee. Colorful! (Serves 6)

Ingredients

1	bunch fresh broccoli, blanched
3	pounds (1½ kg) fresh halibut, cod or haddock, cut into 6 steaks, each about one inch thick
24	dried black olives
24	mussels, well scrubbed

4	tablespoons minced Italian parsley
2	cloves garlic, minced
	Black or cayenne pepper
3	tablespoons olive oil
½	cup dry white wine
	Salt to taste

Method

Blanch the broccoli in boiling water for 3 minutes. Remove to ice water to chill. Lift out with a slotted spoon and set aside. Place the fish steaks in a shallow baking pan. Arrange the olives, mussels and broccoli around the fish. Sprinkle parsley, garlic, black or cayenne pepper, and olive oil over the fish. Add the wine and salt. Cover the pan tightly and cook in a preheated 400°F oven until the mussels open, 5–10 minutes. Serve each slice of fish with vegetables, mussels and wine sauce.

Microwave Instructions

Clean and rinse broccoli. Place in microwave-suitable casserole, cover with plastic wrap and cook for 1–2 minutes on Full Power. Broccoli should be bright green but still crisp. Remove to ice water to chill. Lift out with a slotted spoon and set aside. Place fish steaks in a shallow glass baking dish. Cover with plastic wrap and cook for 6 minutes on Full Power. Turn the steaks over and rearrange. Place olives, mussels and broccoli around the fish. Sprinkle with remaining ingredients. Cover again and cook for 6–8 minutes on Full Power until the mussels open. Serve each slice of fish with vegetables, mussels and wine sauce.

Shrimp with Lemon and Ginger

Cooking teacher Lucy Waverman brought us New Wave cooking—a combination of French and Chinese techniques and flavors. Shrimp sautéed in a frying pan served with a reduced sauce is traditionally French but the ginger, garlic, lemon and shallots transform the best of French into spectacular Sino-French cuisine. Serve these shrimp with boiled fettucine noodles, tossed with a bit of Chinese oyster sauce and a drop of sesame oil. (Serves 6 as an appetizer)

Ingredients

3	slices of peeled fresh ginger, each the size and thickness of a quarter		2	tablespoons butter
			2	shallots or white part of 4 green onions, finely chopped
1	cup dry white wine			
	Rind and juice of half a lemon		1	clove garlic, finely chopped
				Salt and freshly ground pepper
10–14	shrimp, peeled and deveined		¼	cup unsalted butter
2	tablespoons vegetable oil			

Method

Marinate ginger in wine for 2 hours; reserve wine. Cut ginger into thin julienne strips. Remove lemon rind with a vegetable peeler or zester, making sure you discard all white pith. Cut into julienne strips.

Butterfly shrimp by cutting partway through the back vein. At head end, cut right through first ½ inch of shrimp. This makes them stand up.

In a large frying pan, heat oil and 2 tablespoons of butter over high heat until butter mixture sizzles. Sauté shallots and garlic for 1 minute. Add ½ cup of the reserved wine and reduce over high heat until there is no wine left. Add shrimp and sauté for 1 minute. Season with salt and pepper. Scatter in ginger and lemon, stir, then add remaining ½ cup of reserved wine and lemon juice.

Start to reduce the sauce, stirring shrimp. As soon as shrimp are pink and curled, remove with a slotted spoon and arrange on individual serving plates. Boil liquid for another 30 seconds; remove from heat. There should be about 2 tablespoons of liquid left. If not, reduce a little more.

Over very low heat, slowly stir in the ¼ cup of butter, a little at a time. The butter should melt and be incorporated with wine, shallots, ginger and lemon to thicken and enrich the sauce. Do not boil, as this will cause the butter to separate. Shake pan a few times, taste for seasoning and pour over shrimp.

Sauté of Shrimp with Wild Rice, Mushrooms and Tomato

Executive chef Herbert Sonszogni serves this simple main course at his restaurant in Mississauga, Babsi's. It's versatile and you can use regular rice in place of the wild rice and green beans, zucchini or peas in place of the mushrooms. A tip from the chef—cook the shrimp in a very hot pan and do them quickly. Undercook them in the first sauté. That way they stay tender. (Serves 2)

Ingredients

1	tomato, peeled, seeded and chopped	1/2	onion, finely chopped
12	shrimp, cleaned, shelled and deveined	1	clove garlic, finely chopped
		1/2	teaspoon thyme
2	tablespoons olive oil	4	mushrooms, thinly sliced
1/4	teaspoon salt	1/3	cup dry white wine
1/4	teaspoon pepper	4	ounces (100 g) wild rice, cooked
4	tablespoons butter		

Method

Precook rice and keep warm in a steamer over hot water or tossed in butter in a sauté pan. Drop tomato into small pan of boiling water for 15 seconds. Remove with slotted spoon and peel. With sharp knife, cut out and discard core. Cut tomato parallel to the stem and gently squeeze so that the seeds fall out. Now chop finely.

Sauté shrimp quickly in olive oil over high heat—do not overcook at this stage. Season with salt and pepper. Remove from pan and keep warm. Add butter to the same pan and sauté the onion, garlic, thyme, mushrooms and tomato. Add dry white wine and simmer gently for 5 minutes. Adjust seasoning, add shrimp and heat through. Serve immediately over the wild rice.

Note:If prepreparing this dish, undercook the shrimp.

Spaghetti Alla Puttanesca

"Hooker's pasta" is as old as the Roman hills from where it comes. It is salty and fullbodied, much favored by visitors to Italy. No one seems to know why it is named after the great old profession. My theory is that the sauce can be kept for awhile and eaten later—or even eaten cold. It is also a sauce with cheap ingredients—easily affordable by poorly paid people. It uses fish that is plentiful in southern climates—anchovies.

Anchovies are more commonly known to Canadians as a canned fish, while the fresh versions are generally used for bait. The red color of the canned anchovy is not natural but comes from salting and allowing the anchovies to ripen for about 4 months, thus curing the flesh. Anchovy use dates back to the ancient Romans, who took the whole, ungutted fish, put it in brine, and allowed it to ripen in the sun, thus making an all-purpose mash for seasoning that they called garum. (Serves 4)

Ingredients

1	cup pitted, chopped black olives	1	tablespoon parsley, chopped
			Olive oil
5	anchovy fillets, rinsed and mashed	1	can (540 mL) Italian tomatoes, drained and chopped
1	tablespoon capers	1	package (500 g) spaghetti
3	cloves garlic, chopped		

Method

Combine the first 5 ingredients. Heat a small amount of olive oil in a frypan and sauté the olive mixture for 3 minutes. Add the tomatoes and adjust seasonings, adding cayenne if necessary. Cook for about 7 minutes.

Boil a large amount of water with salt. Add the spaghetti and cook till just tender. Drain and immediately add the tomato mixture.

LUNCHEON AND SUPPER MAIN DISHES

Piperade 75

Hunter's Eggs 76

Bridge Club Foamy French Toast 76

Cheese Soufflé for Two 77

Ham and Cheddar Strata 78

Pizza-in-a-Dish 78

Fettucine All'Alfredo 80

Tofu Lasagna 79

Grilled Tofu Sandwich 80

Penne Alla Vodka 81

Quick Spaghetti with Creamy Tomato Sauce 82

Springtime Spaghetti 82

Fresh Tomato, Garlic and Basil Spaghetti 83

Vegetarian Chili 87

Eggplant Casserole 84

Gnocchi di Patate 86

Kasha and Vegetable Pie 85

Piperade

This piperade is wonderful for a quick, simple dinner for 2 or 20; just keep enlarging the quantities. Make it in autumn when the garden vegetables are so plentiful.

If you wish, leave the salt out entirely and substitute herbs and spices—basil, cumin, celery and dill seed in the sauce; ground pepper on the eggs after they're cooked. Serve this to guests—no apologies needed! (Serves 2)

Ingredients

1	tablespoon butter or margarine	½	teaspoon salt (optional) Dash of pepper
1	small clove garlic, chopped	4	eggs
¼	cup chopped onion	2	tablespoons water
¼	cup finely diced green pepper	½	teaspoon salt (optional)
½	cup finely diced celery	1	tablespoon butter or margarine
3	medium tomatoes, chopped	1 or 2	slices thin Swiss cheese

Method

Melt 1 tablespoon butter in saucepan. Sauté garlic, onion, green pepper and celery over medium heat until tender-crisp. Add tomato, ½ teaspoon salt if desired, and pepper. Simmer uncovered for 15 to 20 minutes, stirring occasionally.

Preheat broiler. Five minutes before the sauce is finished, prepare the scrambled eggs: in a small bowl, beat together eggs, water and ½ teaspoon salt. Melt 1 tablespoon butter in frying pan over medium heat. Add eggs and cook until they are set but still moist. Divide eggs evenly between 2 individual casseroles or baking dishes. Top with tomato sauce and Swiss cheese. Broil for 2 minutes or until cheese melts.

Microwave Instructions

In a 4-cup glass measure combine butter, garlic, onion, green pepper and celery. Cook, uncovered for 2–3 minutes on Full Power. Add tomatoes and seasonings. Cook, uncovered for 3–4 minutes on Full Power.

In a 1½-quart glass casserole beat the eggs, water, salt and butter. Cook, uncovered for 5–6 minutes on Medium Power until almost set but still moist, whisking often. Top with tomato sauce and cheese. Cook for 30 seconds to 1 minute on Full Power, until cheese melts.

Hunter's Eggs

I am often surprised by the dishes that are popular with the crew in Studio Seven. Here is an example. Many of them prepared it the following Sunday for brunch or supper and it didn't seem to matter for how many they cooked. For one person or 10, this recipe has it all—taste, color and simplicity! (Serves 4)

Ingredients

¼	cup butter	2	medium tomatoes, blanched,
2	small onions, finely chopped		peeled and sliced
8	chicken livers, cleaned and	4	eggs
	chopped	4	slices hot toast
	Pinch of salt and pepper		

Method

In a non-stick frypan, heat 2 tablespoons of butter. Sauté the onions, livers and a pinch each of salt and pepper, stirring occasionally for 5–7 minutes. Set aside.

Meanwhile, melt the remaining butter in frypan and lightly sauté tomato slices (about 1 minute on each side). Remove and keep warm. Reduce heat to low. Break eggs into pan, and fry for about 4 minutes. Spread chicken-liver mixture over the toast slices, top with a tomato slice and a fried egg and serve immediately.

Bridge Club Foamy French Toast

This is my Mom's bridge club recipe and it's a wow. The trick is to soak the sandwiches ahead of time and cook them just before serving. Then, they puff up like a crusty soufflé in the oven. They must be brought to the table just as they come from the oven, before they fall, for grand effect.

Ingredients

For each serving

2	½-inch thick slices white bread	⅓	cup of milk
1	egg		Pinch of salt

Method

Remove crusts from bread. Place one slice on top of the other and cut the sandwich in half, making certain that the cut edges match exactly. Preheat oven to 325°F.

Beat egg, milk and salt. Dip sandwich in mixture and let soak until all of the liquid is absorbed. Meanwhile, heat a shallow frypan, add a bit of butter or oil and toast sandwich well on each side. Transfer to a cookie sheet. Bake for 15 minutes exactly and serve *immediately*.

The French toast will be light and puffy. Some people like it with strawberry jam, my preference is a dollop of yogurt and a drop of apricot conserve.

Cheese Soufflé for Two

Cooking for two presents its own unique problems and those who master it learn the happy art of simple cooking. A cheese soufflé is one of the nicest dinners to prepare since it leaves time for relaxing, if you wish, between the sauce making and soufflé baking. It's delicious and filling.

Ingredients

1	tablespoon butter	½	cup milk
2	tablespoons flour	½	cup shredded sharp Cheddar cheese
	Pinch of salt and freshly ground black pepper	2	large eggs, separated
	Pinch dry mustard		

Method

Lightly grease a 1-quart soufflé dish. Preheat oven to 350°F. Melt butter over low heat. Blend in flour, salt, pepper and dry mustard. Cook for 1 minute. Gradually add milk, stirring constantly until thickened. Add cheese, stir until melted. Remove from the heat, cool slightly.

Whisk egg yolks together and add a small amount of cheese sauce to the yolks, mixing well, then stir into cheese sauce, stirring to combine. Beat egg whites until stiff but not dry. Fold into cheese sauce. Pour into the prepared pan and bake for 35–40 minutes or until knife inserted in the centre comes out clean.

Microwave Instructions

To make the cheese sauce, melt butter for 30 seconds on Full Power in a 2 or 4-cup glass measure. Blend in the flour and seasonings to make a smooth paste. Cook, uncovered on Full Power for 1 minute. Gradually whisk in the milk until smooth. Cook, uncovered on Full Power 1–2 minutes until the sauce comes to a boil and thickens. Whisk once during cooking. Add cheese, whisk until melted. Bake the soufflé conventionally combining the cheese sauce with the egg yolks and whites gently before baking.

Ham and Cheddar Strata

This looks like a soufflé, but can be prepared a day ahead and baked before serving. And it won't fall! (Serves 6-8)

Ingredients

5	cups French bread, cubed	6	eggs
1½	cups cooked ham, coarsely chopped	3	cups milk
		1	small onion, finely chopped
1	12-ounce (340 g) package frozen spinach, thawed, chopped and drained	½	teaspoon salt
		1	teaspoon dry mustard
2	cups Cheddar cheese, shredded		Pinch cayenne

Method

Grease an 8-cup, deep, straight-sided baking dish. Layer one-third each of the bread, ham, spinach and cheese in the baking dish; repeat to make two more layers.

Beat eggs with milk, onion, salt, mustard and cayenne until blended; pour over strata. Cover and refrigerate at least 3 hours or overnight. Bake uncovered, at 350°F for 1¼ hours or until puffed and golden.

Pizza-in-a-Dish

This is a wonderful budget stretcher. It looks good, tastes great, and can be prepared in advance. It's special enough for company and hearty enough for an after-ski crowd. Add a hot loaf of bread, a crunchy salad and dinner is ready. (Serves 6-8)

Ingredients

10	slices French bread, cubed	2	cups Mozzarella cheese, shredded
2	cups salami, coarsely chopped		
½	cup green pepper, diced (mushrooms and onions may be substituted)	6	eggs
		2½	cups milk
		¾	cup spaghetti sauce

Method

In an 8-cup, deep baking dish, layer one-third each of the bread, salami, green pepper and cheese; repeat to make two more layers. Beat together eggs and milk and pour over casserole. (At this point casserole may be covered and refrigerated overnight if desired.) Drizzle spaghetti sauce over before baking. Bake uncovered at 350°F for 1¼ hours or until puffed and golden.

Tofu Lasagna

Challenge your guests to discover the secret ingredients in this luscious lasagna. It was the surprise hit of the day when our meat-eating crew gathered for lunch. (Serves 6–8)

Ingredients

3	tablespoons oil		Freshly ground black pepper
½	pound (250 g) mushrooms, sliced	1	package (500 g) mashed tofu
2	cloves garlic, crushed	¾	cup grated Parmesan cheese
1	can (796 mL) meatless spaghetti sauce or homemade sauce	½	pound (250 g) Mozzarella cheese, shredded (2 cups)
½	cup wheat germ	¼	cup minced fresh parsley
½	teaspoon salt	6	lasagna noodles, cooked and drained

Method

Heat oil in large frypan, stir in mushrooms and garlic and sauté until softened. Stir in spaghetti sauce, wheat germ, salt and pepper and heat through.

Combine tofu and ½ cup Parmesan cheese in one bowl. Combine Mozzarella cheese and parsley in another bowl.

Preheat oven to 375°F. To assemble spread a thin layer of sauce over the bottom of a 12 × 8 inch baking pan. Place 3 of the lasagna noodles over sauce. Spread half of tofu mixture over noodles evenly, then half of Mozzarella mixture. Spoon half of remaining sauce over, then remaining 3 strips noodles, tofu mixture, then Mozzarella mixture, and finally remaining sauce. Sprinkle evenly with remaining ¼ cup Parmesan cheese.

Bake 20–30 minutes or until cheese melts and dish is thoroughly heated through.

Microwave Instructions

In a 1½-quart microwave container combine oil, mushrooms, garlic and cook 2–3 minutes on Full Power. Stir in spaghetti sauce, wheat germ, salt and pepper and heat 4–6 minutes on Full Power, stirring once. Combine tofu and ½ cup Parmesan cheese in one bowl. Combine Mozzarella cheese and parsley in another bowl. Cook lasagna noodles conventionally. To assemble follow directions above, using a glass 12 × 8 inch pan. Bake, uncovered 5 minutes on Full Power. Rotate dish, if necessary, and cook 10–12 minutes on Medium (50% power) until thoroughly heated through.

Fettucine All' Alfredo

The original recipe is just this—plenty of butter and freshly grated Parmesan cheese tossed well with homemade fettucine. Excellent cooks and food writers have changed it with cream cheese, heavy béchamel sauce and wine but that's incorrect. At Alfredo's restaurant on Via Della Scrofa in downtown Rome, the waiter tosses the delicate noodles in a large bowl at your table, explaining that it is the "triplo burro" and cheese from the heart of the wheel that makes this special. After the toss, he serves each guest and places the tossing bowl in front of the host. It's tradition in food and service that counts. (Serves 4–6)

Ingredients

1	pound (500 g) packaged or homemade fettucine (see Volume I, p. 68–69 for directions) Boiling salted water	1 ⅓–½	cup butter, softened cup Parmesan cheese, grated Freshly ground black pepper

Method

Cook fettucine in boiling salted water until al dente—tender but still firm. Drain. In a warm serving dish put half the softened butter. Add the fettucine, top with remaining butter and sprinkle with Parmesan cheese. Using a fork and spoon, lightly toss the fettucine until well coated and creamy. Sprinkle with freshly ground black pepper. Serve immediately.

Grilled Tofu Sandwich

Here is another tofu recipe that is perfect for lunch or a light snack. The filling is creamy without being high in calories and nutty without tasting rich. This sandwich is unique and we loved it when Margo Oliver prepared it one day for lunch. (Serves 6)

Ingredients

¾	pound (325 g) tofu	½	teaspoon salt
2	tablespoons soybean or other vegetable oil		Black pepper, freshly grated
2	green onions, chopped	12	slices whole-wheat bread
2	tablespoons salted peanuts	½	cup soft butter or margarine
1	tablespoon chopped parsley	¼	cup sesame seeds
1	tablespoon finely chopped celery		

Method

Put all ingredients except whole-wheat bread, butter or margarine and sesame seeds in glass of blender and buzz until smooth. Spread between slices of bread to make 6 sandwiches.

Cream butter or margarine with sesame seeds and spread half the mixture on one side of sandwiches.

Put buttered side down in a hot heavy skillet over moderate heat and cook until browned, then butter second side, turn and brown. Serve hot.

Penne Alla Vodka

Penne is a largish, macaroni-shaped, ribbed pasta that is designed to hold a sauce inside and out. Vodka sauce is the specialty of some Roman restaurants.

Try steeping the red peppers in vodka for several days before preparation and make sure that the dish in which you toss the finished penne is large and hot enough to vigorously toss the penne yet keep it mouth wateringly hot. (Serves 3–4 as an appetizer or 2–3 as a main dish)

Ingredients

1	package (500 g) penne	$\frac{1}{4}$	cup whipping cream
4	quarts water	$\frac{1}{4}$	cup vodka
2	tablespoons butter	1	tablespoon dried red pepper, crushed
1	tablespoon vegetable oil	$\frac{1}{3}$–$\frac{1}{2}$	cup freshly grated Parmesan cheese
$\frac{1}{2}$	cup chopped onion		
2	large tomatoes, peeled and chopped		Parmesan cheese for passing

Method

Steep the pepper in the vodka 3 days before using. Bring the water to the boil in a large pot and add the pasta. Allow it to cook until al dente (approximately 10 minutes, but taste it).

To make the sauce, melt the butter in a saucepan and add the oil. When hot, add the onion and stir well for 5 minutes to soften, not brown. Add the tomatoes and stir. Cook for about 5 minutes. Add the cream and stir to heat. Strain the pepper from the vodka and add the vodka. Simmer for a further 2–3 minutes. Make sure that the serving plate or bowl is hot. Place a bit of the hot sauce in the bottom and turn it around to coat the surface. Drain the penne. Add it to the sauce and toss. Add the balance of the sauce, top with the Parmesan cheese and serve immediately.

Quick Spaghetti with Creamy Tomato Sauce

This is a quick spaghetti dish that is more cream than tomato. If you're serving from a large platter rather than the pan, heat it with boiling water and then dry it; then pour hot sauce on the bottom before adding the spaghetti. Keeps it hot longer. (Serves 6)

Ingredients

5	quarts water	2	tablespoons tomato paste
1½	teaspoons salt	1½	cups Parmesan cheese, freshly grated
1	package (500 g) spaghetti		
1½	cups 10% cream		

Method

In a large pot bring water to a rolling boil. Add the salt and the spaghetti, and stir with a wooden spoon until water returns to a boil.

While spaghetti cooks, pour the cream into a large pan. Heat gently. When the cream is hot, add the tomato paste and stir until dissolved. After the spaghetti is al dente, pour it into the cream mixture and toss vigorously. Add the Parmesan cheese and toss. Pass more cheese with the spaghetti.

Springtime Spaghetti

Pasta primavera owes its birth to an inventive New York chef who dreamed of the perfection of fresh spring vegetables combined with the finest fresh pasta and the choicest fresh cheese. We owe him a debt of gratitude, for this dish, served on an early spring day is a feast to life itself. (Serves 6)

Ingredients

1	cup zucchini, sliced	1	teaspoon minced garlic
1½	cups broccoli, broken into flowerettes	¼	cup Italian parsley, chopped
			Salt and pepper to taste
1½	cups snow peas (optional)	⅓	cup pine nuts
1	cup baby peas	10	large mushrooms, sliced
6	stalks fresh asparagus, if available, sliced	1	package (500 g) spaghetti
5	quarts water	½	cup Parmesan cheese
12	cherry tomatoes, cut in half	1	cup milk
	Oil	⅓	cup chicken stock (optional)
		⅓	cup fresh basil, chopped

Method

Blanch first 5 ingredients in a large pot of boiling water for 5 minutes or until they are tender crisp. Plunge them into a bowl of ice water until cool and then drain. Set aside. This can be done ahead of time. Heat 5 quarts water to boil in the same large pot.

Meanwhile, sauté tomatoes in a little oil with the garlic, salt, pepper and parsley. Remove and set aside. Using the same pan, sauté pine nuts until brown. Now add all of the vegetables, except tomatoes. Add more garlic if desired. Simmer a few minutes until hot.

Drop spaghetti into boiling water. Cook for 8–10 minutes, or until when tasted, al dente. Drain.

Heat oil in a small saucepan, add cheese and milk. Stir to blend and melt cheese. If too thick, thin with chicken stock or milk. Add basil and toss the sauce with the spaghetti. Add ⅓ of the vegetables and toss again. Transfer the spaghetti to a heated platter and top with remaining hot vegetable mixture. Garnish with reserved cherry tomatoes.

Fresh Tomato, Garlic and Basil Spaghetti

Here's Irena Chalmers's ultra-quick pasta sauce that is ready when the pasta is cooked. It's delicious. (Serves 4–6)

Ingredients

1	package (500 g) spaghettini, or any thin pasta	3	large ripe tomatoes, chopped
6	quarts water	3	cloves garlic
2	tablespoons salt	3	teaspoons salt
½	cup olive oil	1	cup fresh basil leaves
			Freshly ground black pepper

Method

Set the water to boil in a large saucepan with 2 tablespoons of salt; this may take half an hour. Add the spaghettini and cook for 7 or 8 minutes, or until tender but firm.

Pour the olive oil into a large serving bowl and add the chopped tomatoes. Mash the garlic with the salt and add. Tear the basil leaves into confetti-sized bits and add, along with the pepper.

Drain the spaghettini, dump it into the bowl, toss thoroughly and serve at once.

Eggplant Casserole

Eggplant is the perfect casserole base as it has a bland taste that seems to heighten the flavors of whatever is added. Here, the sauce is meant to have a mild tomato flavor and if you use herbs carefully will have a slightly sweet flavor, as well. The cheese gives the casserole some zip. Usually fried, the eggplant in this casserole is broiled. (Serves 4)

Ingredients

3	tablespoons oil		and chervil (other herbs may be substituted, but add slowly, tasting at each addition)
1	onion, cut into strips		
2	green peppers, cut into strips		
5	large mushrooms, sliced	1	large eggplant
1	celery stalk, sliced diagonally	2	eggs, beaten with 1 tablespoon water and a pinch of salt
4-5	cloves fresh garlic, minced		
6	tomatoes, peeled and diced		Oil
	Salt (optional)	½	cup grated Parmesan cheese
¼	teaspoon each of dried parsley, tarragon, chives	1	cup shredded Swiss cheese

Method

First prepare the sauce by heating 3 tablespoons oil in large skillet and adding onion, green peppers, mushrooms, celery and garlic. Sauté until tender. Add tomatoes. Bring to a boil. Reduce the heat, cover and simmer for 30 minutes. Add herbs. Taste and adjust seasoning. Remove from heat.

Peel eggplant and slice into large slices. Dip in egg mixture and place on oiled broiler pan. Broil until tender, turning once. Arrange eggplant slices in large baking dish. Sprinkle with Parmesan cheese. Pour tomato sauce over top and sprinkle with Swiss cheese. Heat at 350°F until cheese is melted.

Microwave Instructions

In a 1½-quart (1.5 L) microwave casserole, combine oil, onion, green peppers, mushrooms, celery and garlic. Cook, uncovered 3–5 minutes on Full Power. Add tomatoes, cover and cook 4–5 minutes on Full Power until sauce boils. Stir, then cook 10 minutes on Medium (50% power), stirring occasionally. Add herbs. Let stand. Peel eggplant and slice into large pieces. Omit egg mixture and arrange eggplant slices in a large baking dish. Cover with plastic wrap or waxed paper and steam 5–7 minutes on Full Power until soft. Pour off excess water, pour tomato sauce over and sprinkle with both Parmesan and Swiss cheeses. Bake, uncovered, 4 minutes on Full Power. Rotate, if necessary and cook 8–10 minutes on Medium (50% power), until cheese is melted.

Kasha and Vegetable Pie

A pizza-like vegetarian dinner popular with teenagers. (Serves 4–6)

Ingredients

2	tablespoons butter	1	clove garlic, crushed
1	cup roasted kasha, bulgur, brown rice or other whole-grain cereal	½	pound (250 g) mushrooms, sliced
2	cups boiling water	1½	teaspoons dried oregano
1	tablespoon ketchup	½	teaspoon dried basil
	Salt		Salt and freshly ground black pepper
2	tablespoons oil	1	can (540 mL) tomatoes
1	large onion, chopped	1	cup grated Cheddar cheese
1	green or red pepper, seeded and chopped		

Method

Melt butter in a medium-sized saucepan. Stir in kasha or other grain and cook until thoroughly coated with butter. Add boiling water, ketchup, pinch of salt and bring to a boil. Reduce heat to simmering, cover and cook 10 minutes. Meanwhile, heat oil in large frypan and soften onion and pepper about 5 minutes; do not brown. Add garlic and mushrooms and sauté gently 3–5 minutes. Season with oregano, basil, salt and pepper. Add tomatoes. Stir, cover and leave to simmer gently to reduce the liquid slightly. Stir the cooked buckwheat into vegetable mixture, then spoon into a lightly buttered 9- or 10-inch pie plate or quiche pan. Sprinkle evenly with Cheddar cheese and bake at 375°F for 20–30 minutes, until thoroughly heated through and cheese has melted.

Microwave Instructions

Spoon prepared mixture into a buttered 9- or 10-inch glass pie plate. Sprinkle evenly with Cheddar cheese and bake 6–8 minutes on Medium (50% power), until thoroughly heated through and cheese has melted.

Gnocchi di Patate

Fenton's Restaurant in Toronto has made a name for itself as a first-class restaurant by serving lovely dishes like this one. Gnocchi (dumplings) replace pasta in a traditional Italian meal and chef Werner Bassen makes them light and fluffy with cheese as part of the dough and tomatoes as the key ingredient in the sauce.

If you have a pastry bag, you might try using it for the dough, slicing portions off the end of the nozzle at 1-inch intervals. It is sometimes easier to do it this way than to roll the dough and then slice it. (Serves 6 as an appetizer)

Ingredients

Dough

½	cup water	2	eggs
1	tablespoon butter	2	cups warm mashed potatoes
½	teaspoon salt	½	cup Parmesan cheese, grated
½	cup all-purpose flour	½	cup Gruyère cheese, grated

Sauce

1	tablespoon olive oil	1	cup (250 mL) 35% cream
1	small onion, chopped		Salt and pepper
1	clove garlic, crushed		
2	tomatoes, skinned, seeded and diced		Minced parsley for garnish

Method

Bring water to the boil and add butter and salt. Remove from heat and gradually stir in the flour. Return to heat and beat mixture until dough leaves the sides of the pan. Remove from heat and add the eggs, one by one. Add warm mashed potatoes and cheeses and beat well.

Knead on floured surface until smooth. Divide dough into 4 and roll into long croquettes. Lightly flatten with a fork and cut into 1-inch lengths.

Poach in lightly salted, simmering but not boiling water for about 1 minute or until gnocchi rise to the surface. Remove with a slotted spoon and drop into cold water. Drain well and refrigerate for 1 hour. If not required immediately, the gnocchi may be kept for 2–3 days covered in the refrigerator.

To make sauce, heat the oil and sauté the onion, garlic and tomatoes. Add the cream. Bring to the boil and season to taste with salt and pepper.

Arrange gnocchi on baking dish, cover with sauce and bake for 20–30 minutes in a 350°F oven. Serve sprinkled with chopped parsley.

Microwave Instructions

To make sauce, combine oil, onion, garlic and tomatoes in a 1-quart (1 L) microwave container. Cook, uncovered 2–3 minutes on Full Power. Stir and add cream, salt and pepper. Cook 2–4 minutes on Full Power, until sauce boils, stirring once partway through.

Arrange prepared gnocchi on microwave-safe baking dish, cover with sauce and bake 8–10 minutes on Medium (50% power) until hot for serving. Let stand 5 minutes before serving, then sprinkle with chopped parsley.

Note: If heating cold from refrigerator, cook an additional 4–6 minutes on Medium.

Vegetarian Chili

(Serves 6)

Ingredients

3	tablespoons vegetable oil	2	cans (113 mL) green chilies, drained and chopped
1	cup chopped onion		
1	green or red pepper, cut into strips	½	teaspoon crushed red chilies
		½	teaspoon oregano
2	cloves garlic, minced	1	can (540 mL) kidney beans, drained
1½	cups finely sliced carrots		
1	small zucchini, diced—peel only if old	1	can (340 mL) white canneloni beans, drained (if unavailable use another bean)
½	cup diced celery		
2	cans (398 mL) tomatoes		

Method

Heat the oil in a heavy pan with a lid over medium heat. Add the onion and stir until golden. Add the peppers and garlic. Cook another few minutes, until soft. Stir occasionally and add carrots, zucchini, celery, tomatoes, green and red chilies and oregano.

Simmer for half an hour. Add beans and continue cooking for another half an hour. Taste and adjust seasonings with salt or other spice, if you wish. Serve with rice, whole grain bread or muffins.

VEGETABLES

Artichokes Roman Style 90
Beets in Nippy Cream Sauce 89
Gratin Dauphinois à la Crème 89
Gratin of Greens 90
Vegetable Flan 95
Cooking Tips for Rice 92
Milanese-Style Rice 94
Rice Pilaf 93
Egg and Fried Rice 94

Beets in Nippy Cream Sauce

(Serves 6)

Ingredients

1 tablespoon sugar	Pinch paprika
1 tablespoon prepared horse-radish	1 tablespoon white vinegar
Pinch salt	⅓ cup sour cream or yogurt
	3 cups diced cooked beets

Method

Combine sugar, horseradish, salt, paprika, vinegar and sour cream in saucepan or microwave oven and heat but do not boil. Stir in beets. Heat thoroughly.

Gratin Dauphinois à la Crème

A surprisingly delicious potato casserole. Make it ahead of time and refrigerate it until you're ready to bake it. Chef Roger Dufau suggests this as a complement to his Poulet Basquaise (see p. 51). (Serves 4-6)

Ingredients

1 pound (500 g) potatoes, preferably new	1 cup 35% cream
1 pound (500 g) turnips, sliced	½ cup water
Butter	6 tablespoons Parmesan cheese, grated
Salt and freshly ground pepper	

Method

Peel and slice potatoes and turnips thinly and soak in cold water for 5 minutes. Drain. Butter a gratin dish and place a layer of potatoes on the bottom. Place a layer of turnips overtop and season with salt and pepper. Layer with remaining potatoes and turnips and season again.

Combine cream and water and pour over vegetables to cover. Sprinkle with grated cheese. Cook in 350°F oven for about 35 minutes or until vegetables are done. Cover dish with foil if the top becomes too brown.

Microwave Instructions

Using a large microwave gratin dish, follow above directions, omitting cheese. Bake, covered, 15-18 minutes on Full Power or until vegetables are fork-tender. Sprinkle with cheese and let stand covered 10-15 minutes before serving.

Gratin of Greens

Eat your vegetables this way and love them. Take any green vegetable in your crisper (or combination of greens) and follow the instructions of Jane Rodmell of *Toronto Life Magazine* for a vegetable dish to go along with simple broiled fish or chicken. Use spinach or chard, kale or lettuce. (Serves 4–6)

Ingredients

1   tomato, peeled, seeded and chopped
1   tablespoon olive oil
1   onion, chopped
1   clove garlic, crushed
1   pound (500 g) green vegetables, washed and trimmed
    Salt and freshly ground black pepper

¼   teaspoon marjoram
2   tablespoons freshly grated breadcrumbs
3   egg yolks
½   cup Ricotta cheese
¼   cup Parmesan cheese
    Parmesan cheese, breadcrumbs for garnish

Method

Bring a small pot of water to boil, drop the tomato in for 15 seconds. Remove with slotted spoon, peel, seed and chop. Heat the oil in a skillet or wok and sauté the onion and garlic until soft. Add tomato and greens, turning the mixture over to coat leaves. Sprinkle with salt, pepper and marjoram and stir-fry for 2 minutes. Cover and cook until greens are tender, about 3–5 minutes.

Oil gratin dish and sprinkle with breadcrumbs. Preheat oven to 375°F. Mix together egg yolks and the cheeses. Add to vegetable mixture and stir. Transfer to prepared gratin dish, sprinkle with Parmesan cheese and breadcrumbs and drizzle with oil. Bake for 30 minutes.

Microwave Instructions

Prepare as above, then bake in a microwave gratin dish for 10–12 minutes on Medium (50% power).

Artichokes Roman Style

These marinated artichokes, demonstrated by Signora Jo Bettoia in her Roman kitchen, have become a regular first course in my home. Returning guests now ask that I wait until they arrive before preparing these glamorous vegetables so they may learn the procedure. It's easy to oblige. (Serves 6)

Ingredients

2	lemons, halved	⅔	cup quality olive oil
1½	tablespoons chopped garlic	2	teaspoons salt
2	cups Italian parsley, coarsely chopped	½	teaspoon freshly ground black pepper
10	artichokes	¼	cup dry white wine
¼	cup quality olive oil	1	cup cold water

Essential Equipment

A large bowl of cold water

Heavy saucepan with lid, about 26 inches in diameter

Method

Rub lemon juice onto your hands to avoid darkening the artichoke. Add the juice of 2 lemons to a large bowl of cold water and set aside.

Now you're ready to prepare the artichokes. The harsh, outer, dark green leaves are inedible, so begin to trim them away. Start at the base, pulling the leaves down and twisting them off at the base. Rotate the artichoke as you do this. As the layers are peeled away, you'll begin to notice that the leaves are whitish at the base. Hold each leaf firmly on the white portion and with a tearing motion, rip the leaf tips off. As you rotate the vegetable and move up from the base, you will notice that the leaves are more white than green. Keep working until ⅔ of the vegetable has the whitish color. Then, slice off the green top of the artichoke. This needn't worry you as the green portions are too harsh to eat.

Now, rub the artichoke all over with the cut half of a lemon and begin to trim the stem. As you turn the artichoke over, you'll notice that there is a white centre core in the stem. Trim the green away, leaving the white exposed. If the stem accidentally falls off, slice it close to the base and chop it, adding the bits to the garlic and parsley.

Place the artichokes in the acidulated water as each is cleaned. Combine the garlic and parsley with 1 teaspoon salt, freshly ground black pepper and ¼ cup olive oil. Mix well.

Rub the artichokes back and forth on a wooden cutting board to open them up a little. Place the fingers in the centre and widen the opening. With a demitasse spoon, remove the choke from the centre taking care to remove only the fuzzy part and leave the heart untouched.

In the centre of each artichoke place some of the garlic-parsley-stem mixture. Fill all the artichokes and fit tightly into the heavy saucepan. Sprinkle with 1 teaspoon salt. Drench with ⅔ cup olive oil, dry white wine and 1 cup water. Place on high heat. As soon as the artichokes begin to boil (2 or 3 minutes) cover saucepan and turn heat to medium low. Cook for 40–45 minutes or until the pan "sings," as we say. Remove the cover and cook on high heat until the liquid is absorbed, leaving only oil (about 3–4 minutes). Serve hot or at room temperature.

Cooking Tips for Rice

(Makes 3 cups or 4 servings)

Ingredients

1 cup long-grain rice	¾ teaspoon salt
1¾ cups water or broth	

Method

Place 1 cup of long-grain rice in a heavy 2-quart saucepan with water or broth and salt. Bring quickly to the boil over moderate heat. Reduce heat, cover with tight-fitting lid and simmer gently for 15 minutes or until most of the liquid is absorbed.

Remove pan from the heat. Leave rice in covered pan for 15–20 minutes after it has been cooked. Now remove lid and toss rice lightly with a fork to separate grains. Serve rice as soon as possible after cooking.

To increase quantity

For every 2 cups of long-grain rice, use 3¼ cups water. When preparing more than 2 cups of rice, use a large, heavy, shallow skillet instead of a deep saucepan. This way the rice turns out fluffy and is not compressed by its own weight and volume.

To keep hot

Place rice in covered bowl over saucepan of simmering hot water.

To reheat

Spoon into buttered ovenproof dish, cover with buttered paper and put in a 350°F oven for 30 minutes.

Note 1: Special care is needed in handling rice that has been cooked since the grains mash easily. Rice should never be stirred with a spoon as it will break the grains and make them mushy.

Note 2: Brown rice may be used instead of white rice but increase the amount of water or broth to 2½ cups and double the cooking time. If using converted rice, allow ¼ cup more liquid for each cup of rice. One cup of converted rice makes about 4 cups of cooked rice.

Microwave Instructions

Combine ingredients in a 6 or 8 cup (1.5–2 L) glass casserole. Cover and cook 10–12 minutes on Full Power, stirring halfway through and at the end. Let stand 10–15 minutes before serving. (The rice must be stirred when using the microwave for even penetration of the food.)

Rice Pilaf

Similar to a risotto, the pilaf is a Middle Eastern adaptation of sautéed, flavored rice. Lamb and chicken casseroles are undeniably more tasty when served with a pilaf. (Serves 4–6)

Ingredients

¼ cup butter	½ teaspoon salt
1 medium-sized onion, finely chopped	½ teaspoon black pepper
	3¾ cups hot chicken stock
2 cloves garlic, crushed	1 bay leaf
2 cups long-grain rice	Rind of 1 lemon, thinly pared in one piece
1 cup button mushrooms, wiped clean and sliced	

Garnish

1 tablespoon butter	2 tablespoons raisins
2 tablespoons slivered almonds	

Method

Melt the butter over moderate heat in a saucepan. When the foam subsides, add the onion and garlic and sauté for 5–7 minutes or until the onion is soft and translucent but not brown. Add the rice and cook, stirring constantly, for 5 minutes. Add the mushrooms and cook, stirring constantly, for 3 minutes. Stir in the salt and pepper and pour in the stock. Increase the heat to high and add the bay leaf and lemon rind. When the stock is boiling vigorously, cover the pan, reduce the heat to low and simmer the pilaf for 20–25 minutes, or until the rice is tender and all the liquid has been absorbed.

Meanwhile, in a small frying pan, melt the 1 tablespoon of butter over moderate heat. When the foam subsides, add the almonds and raisins and fry them, stirring constantly, for 5 minutes or until the almonds are lightly browned and the raisins puffed up. Remove the pan from the heat and set aside.

Remove the pilaf from the heat. Remove and discard the bay leaf and the lemon rind. Spoon the pilaf onto a warmed serving platter and scatter the almonds and raisins over the top. Serve immediately.

Milanese-Style Rice

Milanese cooks add beef marrow to this rice dish for taste and fullbodied flavor. I substitute meat glaze. Risotto is to northern Italians what pasta is to southerners—the course to introduce the main dish. Serve it alone and follow it with grilled fish, meat or poultry for a truly Italian meal. (Serves 4–6)

Ingredients

4	tablespoons butter	$\frac{1}{2}$–1	teaspoon saffron
2	ounces (50 g) beef marrow, coarsely chopped or 2 tablespoons meat glaze, if available (see p. 28)	5	cups hot broth, approximately
		2	tablespoons butter
$\frac{1}{2}$	medium onion, minced	$\frac{1}{3}$	cup freshly grated Parmesan cheese—little more for passing
1	pound (500 g) rice, Arborio, if available		Black pepper
$\frac{3}{4}$	cup dry white wine		Salt if necessary

Method

Melt the butter in a saucepan. Add marrow or glaze and stir until dissolved. Add the onion and sauté gently until transparent, about 5 minutes. Add rice and stir until every grain is coated and shiny. Add wine and let it evaporate. Dissolve saffron in 2 tablespoons hot broth and set aside. Add broth, $\frac{1}{2}$ cup at a time, stirring constantly, waiting until broth is absorbed before adding more. After about 15 minutes, taste the rice. It should be al dente. Add saffron and cook for 3 minutes. Remove from the heat, add 2 tablespoons of butter, Parmesan and stir. Cover tightly and allow risotto to set for 3 minutes. Serve with black pepper and more Parmesan if desired.

Egg and Fried Rice

A quick way to use leftover rice. Serve with Chinese Ribs (p. 42). (Serves 4–6)

Ingredients

4	large eggs	$3\frac{1}{2}$	cups cold cooked rice
2	teaspoons salt	2	green onions, chopped
6	tablespoons vegetable oil		

Method

Beat eggs well with ½ teaspoon salt in a large bowl. Heat wok; when hot add 3 tablespoons oil and swirl in wok. Pour in eggs. As they puff around the edges, push cooked eggs to back of wok. Let liquid egg run forward into hot pan. Repeat until eggs are cooked soft and fluffy. Slide into a warm dish and set aside.

Stir rice. Add remaining 3 tablespoons of oil to wok. Add rice, stir-fry to coat with oil. Add remaining salt if needed, stir in eggs, add green onions. Stir-fry a few times.

Vegetable Flan

Luciano, the accomplished chef of Villa d'Este sent along this superb vegetable custard recipe. He serves it with roast beef and everyone finds it luscious. (Serves 4–6)

Ingredients

1½ pounds (700 g) boiled and coarsely chopped spinach and carrots (or any available vegetables)	¼ cup flour
	¼ teaspoon dry mustard
	¼ teaspoon garlic powder
2 cups milk	Freshly ground cayenne
4 eggs	Freshly ground nutmeg
	1 teaspoon salt

Method

Purée all the ingredients in a blender or food processor. Divide mixture into 4–6 individual molds (depending on size). Arrange these in a pan containing water and place in a preheated oven at 375°F for 30–35 minutes.

Microwave Instructions

Arrange microwave molds in a ring formation. Bake 12–16 minutes on Medium (50% power) until just set. Let stand 5 minutes before serving.

SALADS
AND DRESSINGS

Cracked Wheat Salad 97

Mushroom, Spinach and Pepper Salad 98

Mushrooms, Celery and Swiss Cheese Salad 97

Moroccan Carrot Salad 99

Moroccan Cucumber Salad 99

Spinach Salad with Hot Chicken Livers 100

Spinach Salad with Hot Bacon Dressing 100

Hot Sweetbread Salad 102

Hot Potato Salad 101

Winter Salad 101

Cracked Wheat Salad

Irena Chalmers suggests adding leftover ham or chicken to this to make it a main-dish salad. Try chopped fresh mint as a flavor boost, too. (Serves 6)

Ingredients

1	cup cracked wheat	1	cup chopped celery
2	cups boiling water, or enough to cover wheat	1	20-ounce can chick peas, drained, or 2–3 cups of a variety of fresh vegetables, barely cooked
12	scallions, coarsely chopped		
2	medium-sized tomatoes, seeded and cut into small pieces		

Dressing

1	cup parsley, firmly packed	¼	cup lemon juice
3	cloves garlic	½	cup vegetable oil
1	teaspoon Dijon mustard	1	teaspoon salt
1	teaspoon ground coriander		Freshly ground black pepper

Method

Pour the boiling water over the cracked wheat and leave to stand for 30 minutes. Drain. Fluff the wheat by picking up a handful and letting it drift between your fingertips to separate the grains. Add the scallions, tomatoes, celery and chick peas or vegetables.

Meanwhile, combine all the dressing ingredients in a food processor or blender and toss over the salad.

Mushrooms, Celery and Swiss Cheese Salad

This salad may be prepared in the food processor using the slicing blade. Chill or partially freeze the cheese before slicing for uniformity and ease of operation. (Serves 6)

Ingredients

¾	pound (400 g) white button mushrooms	2	tablespoons minced parsley
3	stalks celery	2	tablespoons lemon juice
½	pound package (227 g) Swiss cheese	5	tablespoons olive oil
			Freshly ground pepper to taste
			Salt (optional)

Method

Clean the mushrooms with a damp cloth. Thinly slice stems and caps lengthwise. Chop celery and cut the cheese in strips. Add parsley. Season with lemon juice, olive oil and pepper. Mix and serve.

Mushroom, Spinach and Pepper Salad
(Serves 4)

Ingredients

½ pound (250 g) large mushrooms, thinly sliced and stems
   trimmed
1 tablespoon fresh lemon juice
1 large red or green pepper,
   halved, seeded and thinly
   sliced lengthwise

6 ounces (200 g) Boston lettuce
   leaves, thoroughly washed and
   dried
½ cup spinach leaves, cut,
   washed and dried

Parsley Vinaigrette
(Makes 1 cup)

Ingredients

2 tablespoons fresh parsley
   leaves
1 small shallot
⅜ cup oil

2 tablespoons red wine vinegar
¼ teaspoon salt or to taste
   Freshly ground pepper

Method

Combine sliced mushrooms, lemon juice and pepper and chill until serving time. Prepare lettuce and spinach and keep in refrigerator. Mix vinaigrette ingredients together. Just before serving, toss lettuce, spinach, mushroom and pepper with vinaigrette. Serve immediately.

Moroccan Carrot Salad

Marinated salads take the rush out of meal planning. This one can use tasteless storage carrots in the middle of winter and return them to the flavor of the tropics. (Serves 4)

Ingredients

2	pounds (1 kg) carrots, cleaned and sliced thinly	2	cloves garlic, minced
1	teaspoon salt	8	tablespoons vegetable oil
½	teaspoon ground cumin	2	tablespoons lemon juice or white vinegar
½	teaspoon chili powder	2	tablespoons chopped fresh coriander or parsley
½	teaspoon paprika		

Method

Drop carrots into boiling water and cook for 15 minutes or until soft. Remove them with a slotted spoon. Save some of the cooking liquid. Combine the balance of the ingredients and marinate the carrots in this mixture for 24 hours in refrigerator. Taste and adjust the seasoning. Add carrot liquid if necessary to thin the marinade. Serve chilled.

Moroccan Cucumber Salad

Here's a slightly different cucumber salad that combines spices and tomatoes with the greens. Serve it with marinated roasted lamb leg or rabbit with honey and tomato. (Serves 6)

Ingredients

2	large cucumbers, peeled, cut in half lengthways, seeded and cut into ½-inch pieces	4	tablespoons olive oil
		1	tablespoon vinegar
2	medium tomatoes, blanched, peeled, seeded and roughly cut	½	teaspoon ground cumin
		½	teaspoon salt
1	medium-sized onion, quartered and sliced	¼	teaspoon dried thyme

Method

Prepare vegetables and toss together. Prepare dressing combining oil, vinegar and spices. Toss all together and taste. Adjust seasonings, if necessary.

Spinach Salad with Hot Chicken Livers

Françoise Monnet, the young chef of Les Parisiennes Restaurant in Toronto features hot salads for luncheon. They are light but filling and judging by the response of the customers, very popular. (Serves 6)

Ingredients

2	pounds (1 kg) fresh spinach		2	teaspoons Dijon mustard
3	tablespoons honey		2	tablespoons red wine vinegar
½	cup milk		6	tablespoons peanut oil
1	pound (500 g) chicken livers			Salt to taste
4	ounces (100 g) mushrooms, sliced			Freshly ground white pepper
2	firm tomatoes, sliced		2	tablespoons clarified butter

Method

Wash the spinach thoroughly under cold running water. Remove the stems. Dry and break leaves into bite-size pieces. Combine honey and milk, add cleaned chicken livers and marinate for 3 hours. Combine spinach leaves, sliced mushrooms and tomatoes in a salad bowl.

Prepare dressing by combining together in a separate bowl, mustard, vinegar, peanut oil and seasonings.

Sauté the chicken livers in the clarified butter until cooked but not dry. Arrange them over the spinach and pour over the dressing.

Spinach Salad with Hot Bacon Dressing

A wonderfully tasty first course or luncheon dish. Add more egg if you serve it as the main course. (Serves 2-4)

Ingredients

4	cups spinach leaves, washed and trimmed		1	cup bean sprouts, washed

Dressing

1	cup cider vinegar		¼	cup sugar
¼	cup water			

Garnish

½	cup croutons		5	slices bacon, drained and crumbled
1	hard-boiled egg, grated			

Method

Combine spinach and bean sprouts. Heat vinegar, water and sugar together until sugar is dissolved. Pour over the salad immediately. Garnish with croutons, bacon and grated egg.

Hot Potato Salad

(Serves 4–6)

Ingredients

2	pounds (1 kg) potatoes		Salt to taste
2	teaspoons Dijon mustard		Freshly ground pepper
¼	cup shallots, chopped	7	tablespoons peanut oil
3	tablespoons tarragon vinegar		

Method

Scrub and boil potatoes in their skins for about 10 minutes. *Note:* Be careful not to overcook the potatoes for this salad—they should retain their firmness or they will turn mushy when the dressing is added. Drain and peel when cool enough to handle. Cut into slices.

In a separate bowl, combine Dijon mustard, chopped shallots, vinegar, salt and pepper. Add the peanut oil last and slowly, little by little. Mix well.

Pour dressing over potatoes while they are still warm. Toss gently and leave to stand for about 1 hour before serving to allow potatoes to absorb flavor. Serve at room temperature.

Winter Salad

(Serves 4–6)

Ingredients

1	large sweet red pepper		small pieces
¼	pound (100 g) ham, in one slice	3	apples, diced (leave skins on)
1	bunch (1¼ pounds—600 g) broccoli, washed and cut into	3	tablespoons lemon juice

Dressing

1	tablespoon Dijon mustard	3	tablespoons chopped parsley
4	tablespoons vegetable oil		Pinch of white pepper
3	shallots, peeled and chopped	12	walnut halves to garnish

Method

Wash pepper, cut in half lengthwise, remove stem and seeds and cut into strips. Dice the ham. Steam for 5 minutes with the broccoli. Chill. Core and dice the apples into a bowl. Toss them with the lemon juice.

To prepare the dressing mix the mustard well with the vegetable oil in a salad bowl. Add the shallots, parsley and pepper and toss well.

Add the broccoli, pepper and ham, then the apples. Mix carefully. Garnish with walnuts and serve at once.

Hot Sweetbread Salad

(Serves 4–6)

Ingredients

2	pounds (1 kg) sweetbreads	½	pound (225 g) carrots
2	tablespoons butter		Snow peas and asparagus for
2	medium-sized celeriac		garnish
½	pound (225 g) leeks		

Dressing

3	tablespoons raspberry vinegar		Salt to taste
1	tablespoon shallots, chopped finely		Freshly ground white pepper
		9	tablespoons peanut oil

Method

Prepare sweetbreads by soaking in cold water for about 1 hour. Blanch them for 10 minutes in boiling salted water. Drain and cool, trim lengthwise into 2-inch slices. Sauté for 2 minutes on each side in melted butter.

Peel the celeriac to remove outer skin. Cut celeriac, leeks and carrots into julienne strips and blanch them for 3 minutes in boiling, salted water. Drain and cool. Blanch snow peas and asparagus separately and set aside.

Mix together the raspberry vinegar, shallots and season to taste with salt and freshly ground white pepper. Add oil slowly and beat with a fork.

Mix half the dressing with the vegetables and arrange on serving dish. Place the sweetbreads on the top of vegetables and pour remainder of dressing overall. Decorate with blanched snow peas and asparagus.

BREADS

Whole-Grain Buttermilk Bread 104

Bagels 106

Croissants 108

Baking Powder Biscuits 106

Gruyère Garlic Bread 107

Pita Bread 105

Whole-Grain Buttermilk Bread

This recipe makes a most delicious whole-grain bread. It is slightly sweet, the texture is fine and the crust is crunchy. We use it to complement a vegetable casserole or stew or for breakfast with fresh marmalade. (Makes 3 loaves)

Ingredients

1¼ cups 5-grain cereal (Red River is a good example)

1½ cups boiling water

2 packages (8 g) active dry yeast

1 cup buttermilk

¼ cup vegetable oil

¼ cup liquid honey

1 tablespoon salt

3 cups whole-wheat bread flour (sold as hard-wheat flour)

3 cups all-purpose flour

1 cup all-purpose flour, for kneading

Oil or melted butter for brushing on loaves and in pans during baking

1 egg mixed with 1 tablespoon water for brushing loaves

Method

Combine the cereal and boiling water in a large bowl and let stand for at least one hour. Prepare the yeast as described on the package. It will rise and become frothy.

Add the yeast mixture, buttermilk, oil and honey to the cereal. Stir well to combine the mixture smoothly. Add salt, 1 cup of whole-wheat flour and 1 cup of the white flour and beat well to combine. Add the 2 remaining cups of each of the flours and beat until smooth. Dough should be uniform and leave the sides of the bowl. It will take about 10 minutes, depending upon the strength of your arm.

When the dough is ready to be kneaded—smooth and pliable— remove from the bowl onto a lightly floured surface and knead for 10–15 minutes. *If using a kitchen machine* with a dough hook, keep it at speed 3 and beat for 10 minutes—this includes kneading time.

Spread a large, clean bowl with oil; put the dough in it, turning it over so that the entire surface is coated. Let it rise, covered, until doubled. It can be left in the refrigerator overnight now.

If refrigerated, bring dough out and allow it to come to room temperature. Punch the dough down and let it rest, covered, on board for 10 minutes. Spread 3 loaf pans with melted butter. The best size for the pans is 9 × 5 inches.

Divide the dough in thirds, roll into loaf shape and place in the pans. Cover them with a damp towel and allow them to rise for an hour or until double in bulk. Heat the oven to 350°F. Bake for 30 minutes. Remove loaves from the oven and brush with the egg mixture. Bake for another 15 minutes. Remove from the pans. Cool on a rack.

Pita Bread

Popular as a sandwich bread and accompaniment to Middle Eastern curries and salads, pita bread is available in commercial bakeries. This homemade version of Margo Oliver is so much lighter and tastier that you may never buy another one again. (Makes 8)

Ingredients

½	cup warm water	2	teaspoons salt
2	teaspoons sugar	¼	cup olive oil
2	packages (8 g) dry yeast	1¾	cups warm water
7	cups all-purpose flour		Cornmeal

Method

Put the ½ cup warm water in a medium bowl. Add sugar and stir to dissolve. Sprinkle yeast over and let stand 10 minutes. Stir well.

Mix flour and salt in a large bowl. Make a well in centre and add yeast mixture, oil and 1¾ cups warm water. Gradually beat flour into liquids, adding a little more warm water if necessary to make a firm ball. Mix with a spoon, then with hand. Turn out onto a floured board and knead until very smooth and elastic, 15–20 minutes. Shape into a ball.

Put dough in a large oiled bowl and turn over so the top is oiled, too. Cover with a damp cloth and let rise in a warm place until double, about 1 hour.

Punch dough down and divide into 8 equal pieces. Shape each piece into a ball and put on a lightly floured board. Cover again with a damp cloth and let rise 30 minutes.

Lightly grease 2 large cookie sheets and sprinkle generously with cornmeal. Roll 4 of the dough balls into circles 8 inches in diameter and about ⅛ inch thick. (The other 4 dough balls will be used when these are baked.) Put 2 of these rounds on opposite corners of each cookie sheet, leaving a little space between them. Cover with a towel and let stand 30 minutes.

While the dough is rising, arrange oven racks so one is at bottom of oven and the other just above the centre. Heat oven to 500°F.

Bake one sheet of breads on lower rack 5 minutes. Move to upper rack and bake until puffed and browned, about 5 minutes more. Remove breads from cookie sheet and slip into plastic bags or wrap loosely in foil to keep moist and pliable—do not seal closed. Bake second sheet of breads and wrap the same way. Repeat rolling, rising and baking with remaining 4 dough rounds.

Wrap cooled bread airtight to store or freeze. To reheat, wrap in foil and place in a 400°F oven 10–15 minutes.

Baking Powder Biscuits

These biscuits are quick and versatile. They can be served hot from the oven with very little fuss or used as a quick topping for a stew or pot pie. There are a few tricks to making them. Because there is quite a bit of liquid relative to the flour, they need light handling. Mix them briefly, and then knead them lightly until they are no longer nobby to touch nor sticky—about 20 turns should do it. Then let them rest. Cut them with a sharp cutter so that they are uniformly cut and will rise evenly. (Makes 24 biscuits)

Ingredients

2	cups all-purpose flour	6	tablespoons vegetable shortening or unsalted butter, chilled
1	tablespoon baking powder		
½	teaspoon salt	⅔	cup milk

Method

Food processor
Insert steel knife. Place flour, baking powder and salt in work bowl and combine briefly. Add shortening (or butter) and mix using ON/OFF turns until shortening is size of small peas. With machine running pour milk into feed tube; stop as soon as dough is mixed. Do not overmix.

Hand method
In mixing bowl, combine flour, baking powder and salt. Cut in shortening until size of small peas. Add milk all at once and stir until dough clings together. On floured surface, toss dough lightly to coat with flour. Knead 12–15 times.

Turn dough out onto well-floured surface and let it rest under an inverted bowl for 20 minutes. Now, heat the oven to 450°F. After 20 minutes, remove bowl and roll out the dough to ½-inch thickness. Cut into 1½-inch rounds using a biscuit or cookie cutter. Transfer to ungreased baking sheet. For soft-sided biscuits, rounds should be almost touching. For crustier biscuits, space one inch apart. Bake 10–15 minutes or until golden brown.

Bagels

There are some people who believe that smoked salmon and cream cheese were invented exclusively for bagels. (Makes 12 bagels)

Ingredients

4½	cups all-purpose flour, approximately	1½	cups warm water (110°F)
1	package (8 g) active dry yeast	1	tablespoon sugar
		1	tablespoon salt

Method

In a large mixer bowl, combine 1½ cups of the flour and the yeast. Combine water, sugar, and salt. Add to dry mixture in mixer bowl. Beat at low speed with electric mixer for ½ minute, scraping sides of bowl constantly. Beat 3 minutes at high speed. By hand, stir in enough of the remaining flour to make a moderately stiff dough. Turn out onto lightly floured surface and knead until smooth and elastic (8–10 minutes). Cover; let dough rest 15 minutes.

Roll dough until 12 inches long, then divide into 12 one-inch lengths. Shape into smooth balls. Punch a hole in centre of each with a floured finger. Pull gently to enlarge hole, working each bagel into a uniform shape. Cover; let rise 20 minutes. Place raised bagels on ungreased baking sheet and broil 5 inches from heat for 1½–2 minutes on each side.

In a large kettle combine 1 gallon water and 1 tablespoon sugar; bring to boil. Reduce heat to simmering; cook 4 or 5 bagels at a time for 7 minutes, turning once. Drain. Place on greased baking sheet. Bake at 375°F for 25 minutes.

Gruyère Garlic Bread

A very special bread to serve with soup or casserole dinners.
(Makes 2 loaves)

Ingredients

1	tablespoon sugar	2	cups all-purpose flour, approximately
1½	cups warm water		
1	package (8 g) active dry yeast	½	teaspoon white pepper
1	tablespoon salt	¾	cup grated Gruyère cheese
2	tablespoons garlic, finely chopped	1	egg white, beaten with 1 tablespoon water

Method

Dissolve sugar in warm water and sprinkle yeast over the top. Let it sit for 10 minutes. Combine salt, garlic and flour. Add the yeast mixture and blend. Add more flour if necessary to make a manageable dough. Turn dough onto a lightly floured surface and knead a few minutes. Sprinkle the pepper over the dough and knead a few more minutes. Add cheese and knead dough until it is smooth and elastic. Place the dough in a greased bowl, place in a plastic bag and let rise in a warm spot until double the bulk. A large measuring cup is good for rising dough as you can read the measures as it rises. When it is double in volume, it is ready.

After the dough has risen, punch down then set aside to rise again until double in bulk. Punch down and place dough on a board. Divide in half, shaping each half into a free form on a lightly greased cookie sheet. Cover with a clean towel and let rise. Lightly brush the top with combined egg white and water. Bake in a preheated 350°F oven for 40–50 minutes or until done.

Croissants

Once you've tried a home-baked buttery rich yeast croissant, nothing else will do. Finding and perfecting a recipe isn't easy but when the right combination finally gels, there is a real sense of accomplishment. In my search for the perfect croissant, I tested recipes from west coast to east. Finally, with a tip from master baker Meta McCall, these croissants emerged. They are simple to make, in my opinion, and as a basic roll are adaptable according to your menu. The secret that turned failure into success was to use cake yeast instead of granular yeast and thereby keep the dough cold during the rolling and turning. Thank you Meta. (Makes 21 croissants)

Ingredients

2¼ cups all-purpose flour	2 tablespoons very soft butter (optional)
3 tablespoons sugar	
1½ teaspoons salt	¾ cup unsalted butter, moderately soft
¾ cup cold milk	
1 package (25 g) compressed cake yeast	1 egg and 1 tablespoon water for egg glaze

Method

Measure and combine flour, sugar and salt. Mix and blend together the cold milk, yeast and soft butter, if using. Add the liquid ingredients to the dry, stirring to blend. Work the cold dough until it can be turned out onto a board or marble slab—about 5–6 kneading motions. Turn the dough onto the board and allow it to rest for 2 or 3 minutes.

Knead the dough lightly—just to form a firm dough—about 10 times. The dough should feel smooth and strong enough to hold together but not so strong that it will be difficult to handle.

Cover the dough with an inverted bowl and leave for about an hour. The dough will have relaxed and can be rolled out to an 8 inch × 10 inch rectangle. Fold in three, left side into the middle and right side over these folds, just like a business letter. Wrap in plastic wrap and place in the refrigerator until quite chilled. Meanwhile, remove the unsalted butter from the refrigerator and let it warm up between sheets of waxed paper.

When the dough is cold, bang it with a rolling pin until it is flat and smooth. It must be malleable but not greasy. If it threatens to be too soft, refrigerate and start again when chilled. It should be a flat rectangle.

Remove the folded dough from the refrigerator and pat or roll it until it measures about 14 × 8 inches. Lay the flattened butter over the upper two-thirds of the cold dough, leaving a narrow dough border around it. Then fold the dough again like a letter, bringing the unbuttered dough over and covering it with the buttered side. There will be 3 layers of dough with 2 layers of butter between. That was turn 1.

For turn 2, turn the dough so that the fold is on your left side as though the dough were a book. Roll the dough until it is again a rectangle 14 × 8 inches and fold in three. Wrap in plastic wrap and refrigerate.

The third turn is done after the dough is very chilled. If you want to leave it in the refrigerator until the next day, place a heavy object on it to weigh it down. If you wish to continue, wait 2 hours. Roll the dough again to a large rectangle, fold in three. Roll the dough out to about $\frac{1}{8}$ inch thick. Cut the dough in three across the width. Refrigerate the dough you aren't using.

Spread parchment paper on baking sheets. Cut the dough into 7 triangles. Roll each triangle from the wide end to the narrow and place the crescents onto the baking sheet. Place a wine glass at each corner of the baking sheet to support a towel-cover. Leave dough under this tent to rise for $\frac{1}{2}$–$\frac{3}{4}$ hour. Mix egg with water to form egg glaze and brush crescents. Bake in a 375°F preheated oven for 15 minutes. Cool on a rack for 15 minutes before serving.

Continue the rising, glazing and baking instructions for the balance of the dough.

To freeze: It is best to freeze the croissants after they are baked. Just warm them in the oven for a few minutes before serving.

MUFFINS, CAKES AND COOKIES

Applesauce Bran Muffins 111

Apple Muffins 111

Best Bran Muffins 112

Carrot-Pineapple Muffins 112

Carrot-Honey Bran Muffins 113

Whole-Wheat Corn Muffins 114

Whole-Wheat Pumpkin Muffins 114

Apricot Upside Down Cake 116

Yogurt Coffee Cake 115

Danish Pastry 118

Chocolate Cake 117

Twice-Baked Hazelnut Cookies 119

Rolled Almond Cookies 120

Holiday Refrigerator Cookies 121

Applesauce Bran Muffins
(Makes 12 muffins)

Ingredients

¼	cup oil	½	cup raisins
½	cup lightly packed brown sugar	1	cup all-purpose flour
2	eggs, lightly beaten	2½	teaspoons baking powder
⅓	cup milk	½	teaspoon salt
⅔	cup applesauce	½	teaspoon cinnamon
1	cup natural bran	¼	teaspoon cloves
		¼	teaspoon nutmeg

Method

Preheat oven to 400°F. Lightly grease muffin pans. In medium-sized bowl combine oil, sugar, eggs, milk and applesauce; beat well. Stir in bran and raisins.

Combine dry ingredients and stir into liquid all at once. Stir only enough to moisten. Fill greased muffin pans two-thirds full with batter. Bake for 20 minutes.

Apple Muffins
(Makes 12–14 large muffins)

√ good

Ingredients

2	eggs	⅛	teaspoon nutmeg
1	cup milk	2	medium apples, peeled, cored and finely chopped (about 2 cups)
2	tablespoons melted butter		
¼	cup sugar	½	cup raisins
2	cups whole-wheat flour	¼	cup sugar
¼	teaspoon salt	¼	teaspoon cinnamon
4	teaspoons baking powder		
¼	teaspoon cinnamon		

Method

Preheat oven to 375°F. Grease muffin cups. Beat eggs, milk, butter and ¼ cup sugar well. Combine flour, salt, baking powder, cinnamon and nutmeg. Mix with a fork. Stir in apples and raisins. Spoon into prepared muffins cups. Mix remaining sugar and cinnamon together and sprinkle over muffins. Bake for 25–30 minutes.

Best Bran Muffins

A successful bran muffin never lingers on the plate. It usually vanishes within minutes of baking. Here is a recipe for fast-disappearing bran muffins. For special occasions, include some walnuts with the raisins. (Makes 12 large muffins)

Ingredients

¼	cup vegetable oil	1½	cups natural bran (sold in bulk—not as a cereal)
¼	cup molasses	1	cup all-purpose flour
⅓	cup honey	1½	teaspoons baking powder
2	eggs, lightly beaten	½	teaspoon baking soda
¾	cup milk (don't skimp here, a little more is better than a little less)	½	teaspoon salt
		½	cup or more raisins

Method

Preheat the oven to 375°F. Prepare muffin tins with paper liners or by brushing each one lightly with melted butter. Combine oil, molasses, honey, eggs and milk in a medium-sized bowl, mixing well. Stir in the bran. Measure the raisins and, if using nuts, measure them, too.

Combine the flour and other dry ingredients. Add these to the liquid ingredients and bran, stirring with a very few swift strokes—only for about 15 seconds. The dough will be lumpy. *Do not overmix.*

Add the raisins. Measure the batter into the tins using an ice cream scoop or measuring cup for even-sized muffins. They should be two-thirds full.

Bake for 15–20 minutes or until a toothpick comes out clean. Serve warm with butter and jam or just as they come from the oven.

Carrot-Pineapple Muffins

So moist, they don't need butter. (Makes 12 large muffins)

Ingredients

1–1½	cups all-purpose flour	2	eggs
1	cup sugar	⅔	cup vegetable oil
1	teaspoon baking powder	1	cup raw carrots, grated
1	teaspoon baking soda	½	cup crushed pineapple with juice
1	teaspoon ground cinnamon		
½	teaspoon salt	1	teaspoon vanilla

Method

Preheat oven to 350°F. Lightly grease muffin tins. Measure the ingredients. Combine the flour, sugar, baking powder and soda, cinnamon and salt in a large bowl. In a smaller bowl, lightly beat the eggs. Add oil, carrots, pineapple and vanilla to eggs, blending well. Pour liquid mixture into dry ingredients, stirring until just blended. Do not beat or overmix.

Spoon batter into muffin tins until about two-thirds full. Bake 20–25 minutes, or until golden brown.

Carrot-Honey Bran Muffins

(Makes 12 muffins)

Ingredients

1½ cups unprocessed wheat bran (not cereal)	½ cup chopped walnuts or almonds
¼ cup wheat germ	1 cup raisins or chopped dates, figs or prunes
1 cup whole-wheat flour	
1 teaspoon baking powder	1 egg, slightly beaten
1 teaspoon baking soda	¾ cup milk
½ teaspoon salt	½ cup honey
1 cup shredded carrots	3 tablespoons salad oil

Method

Preheat oven to 400°F. Stir together bran, wheat germ, flour, baking powder, soda and salt in a mixing bowl. Add carrots, nuts and dried fruit. Mix to distribute evenly. Make well in centre of mixture. Combine egg with milk, honey and oil. Add all at once to flour mixture. Stir to moisten. Spoon into greased or paper-lined muffin pan cups, filling about ¾ full. Bake for 15–20 minutes or until done. Serve warm with Honey Butter.

Honey Butter

Whip together 1 part mild-flavored honey and 2 parts soft butter. Store in refrigerator.

Whole-Wheat Corn Muffins

If an extra guest arrives at short notice, I make corn muffins. They stretch the main course admirably and their crunchy texture and delicious flavor add immeasurably to the meal. (Makes 12 muffins)

Ingredients

1	cup whole-wheat flour
1	cup cornmeal
2	teaspoons baking powder
½	teaspoon salt

1	cup milk (skim milk will do fine)
4	tablespoons vegetable oil
2	tablespoons honey

Method

Preheat the oven to 400°F. Spread the muffin tins with soft butter or margarine. (Oil may be used but I prefer the taste of butter). Blend the dry ingredients together in a large bowl. Beat and combine the liquid ingredients together in a small bowl. Quickly add these to the dry ingredients and stir just until the flour is moistened; there should be no extra beating here. The batter will be lumpy, but check that there are no pockets of flour at the bottom of the bowl.

Drop by spoonfuls into the prepared tins. Make sure that the muffin cups are no more than two-thirds full. Bake for 25 minutes or until they are browned and springy to the touch. Run the point of a sharp knife around each muffin, then cool on a rack.

Microwave Instructions

Place paper liners in microwave muffin pans or 6 small custard cups. Fill two-thirds full. Arrange custard cups in a circle in the microwave and bake for 1½–2½ minutes on Full Power. (This is for 6 muffins.) Test with a toothpick to determine if they are done. Remove muffins from the pan or custard cups and allow them to cool. Repeat with remaining batter.

Whole-Wheat Pumpkin Muffins

(Makes 12–14 large muffins)

Ingredients

1½	cups whole-wheat flour
1½	teaspoons baking powder
½	teaspoon baking soda
½	teaspoon salt
½	teaspoon cinnamon
¼	teaspoon nutmeg
	Pinch of ground cloves

2	eggs
¾	cup cooked & mashed or canned pumpkin
½	cup vegetable oil
½	cup brown sugar
¼	cup orange juice or milk
¼	cup honey

Method

Preheat oven to 400°F and lightly grease muffin tins. Combine flour, baking powder and soda, salt and spices in large bowl. Lightly beat eggs in a small bowl and stir in remaining ingredients until well combined. Pour liquid ingredients into dry ingredients and stir only until blended. Do not beat or overmix. Spoon into muffin tins, about two-thirds full. Bake 20 minutes, or until toothpick in centre comes out clean.

Yogurt Coffee Cake

This is probably one of the simplest cakes to make and serve. The streusel topping is a lovely replacement for icing and the texture of the cake makes it fancy enough for guests. Great with coffee or tea.
(Makes 16 squares)

Ingredients

1	cup yogurt	1	teaspoon vanilla
1	teaspoon baking soda	1¾	cups cake and pastry flour
½	cup butter	1	teaspoon baking powder
1	cup sugar	¼	teaspoon salt
2	eggs		

Topping and Filling

¼	cup brown sugar	1	teaspoon cinnamon
2	tablespoons crushed nuts		

Method

Preheat oven to 350°F. Combine yogurt and baking soda and let stand. Cream butter and sugar, then beat in eggs until light and fluffy. Add vanilla.

Combine flour, baking powder and salt. Add to butter mixture alternately with yogurt, beginning and ending with flour mixture.

Pour half of batter into a lightly greased and floured 8- or 9-inch pan, add half of topping, the rest of the batter, then the topping. Bake for 30 to 40 minutes or until a toothpick inserted in the centre comes out clean. Allow to cool in the pan. Cut into squares.

Microwave Instructions

Prepare as directed. Pour the batter into an ungreased 8- or 9-inch (20 cm or 23 cm) round glass baking dish. Bake 6 minutes on Medium (50% Power), rotate if necessary and bake 1–3 minutes on Full Power until a toothpick inserted near the centre comes out clean. Allow cake to cool in the pan.

Apricot Upside Down Cake

When the oven is on and an inspiration for dessert escapes you, try a simple upside down cake. Sometimes the oldest ideas are still the best.

Ingredients

¼-½	cup butter or margarine		1	teaspoon baking powder
½-1	cup brown sugar		4	egg yolks
1	cup pecan or walnut halves		1	tablespoon butter, melted
1	10-ounce can (284 mL) apricots, packed in juice		1	teaspoon vanilla
			4	egg whites
1	cup cake and pastry flour		1	cup sugar

Method

Preheat the oven to 350°F. In an 8-inch (1 L) round or square baking pan melt the butter and add the brown sugar. When they are blended together remove from heat and arrange the fruit and nuts overtop. Combine the flour and baking powder in a large bowl. Combine the melted butter and vanilla with the egg yolks in a small bowl. Whip the egg whites until stiff but not dry and gradually add the sugar, beating constantly.

Gradually add the yolk mixture to the whites by folding gently and then add flour and baking powder in 4 additions, very carefully. Pour the batter over the fruit and nuts in the pan and bake for half an hour.

Immediately after removing the pan from the oven, invert it over a serving plate. Leave the pan a minute or two so that the brown sugar mixture will flow down and onto the cake.

Remove the pan and serve warm with vanilla ice cream or whipped cream if you wish.

Microwave Instructions

Melt the butter for 1½ minutes on Full Power in an 8- or 9-inch (20 cm or 23 cm) round glass pan. Add the brown sugar and follow above directions.

Elevate the pan in the microwave oven on a custard cup or roasting rack. Bake 6 minutes on Medium (50% Power). Rotate the pan if necessary and bake 1-3 minutes on Full Power until a toothpick inserted near the centre comes out clean. Let stand 5 minutes before inverting onto a serving plate.

Chocolate Cake

You probably have a copy of this cake somewhere in your recipe books. If not, allow me to introduce you to the first genuine bake-in-the mixing-pan cake. No chocolate to melt, no expensive nuts to buy—just everyday home ingredients. (Serves 8)

Ingredients

⅓	cup cocoa	2	teaspoons vanilla
1	cup granulated sugar	½	cup vegetable oil
1½	cups all-purpose flour	1	cup water
1	teaspoon baking soda	2	tablespoons vinegar
½	teaspoon salt		

Method

Preheat the oven to 375°F. Measure all of the ingredients except the vinegar into a square 8-inch (20 cm) pan. Stir well with a fork. Add the vinegar quickly, mixing to combine all ingredients together and immediately place the pan in the oven. Bake for 20–25 minutes or until the cake begins to leave the sides of the pan.

If you prefer chocolate cakes with icing, break a plain chocolate bar into squares, melt it and spread overtop of the warm cake. Or simply press some icing sugar through a sieve over the top of the cake after it has cooled.

Microwave Instructions

Prepare recipe as directed above in a *round* glass 8- or 9-inch (20 cm or 23 cm) baking dish. Elevate in microwave and bake for 6 minutes on Medium (50% Power). Rotate, if necessary, and bake 1–3 minutes on Full Power, until a toothpick inserted near the centre comes out clean. Let stand 5–10 minutes.

Danish Pastry

When professional baker Meta McCall prepared her Danish pastry a hush fell over Studio 7. Everyone knows how delicious these airy, rich pastries can be; no one imagined that they could be simple to prepare. With a few secrets revealed, we all felt confident that we could duplicate her luscious Danish pastries.

Cake yeast mixed in with cold milk replaces the regular granular yeast to keep the dough cold enough for the butter layers to stay locked in between the dough. If the dough warmed enough to feel sticky, Meta popped it into the refrigerator to chill.

Fill the pastries with cherry or apple pie filling or simply spread with honey and nuts and bake. (Makes three 14-inch filled pastries)

Ingredients

¼ cup unsalted vegetable shortening or butter at room temperature

2 tablespoons sugar

1 teaspoon salt

2 small eggs

1½ (25 g) squares compressed cake yeast

¾ cup cold milk

2 cups all-purpose flour

1 cup pastry flour

1 (225 g) package butter

Brown sugar and butter

1 egg mixed with 1 tablespoon water for wash

Sliced almonds and sugar to decorate

Method

In a large dry mixing bowl mix shortening and sugar together. Add salt. Blend in eggs one at a time. Dissolve yeast in cold milk and add to bowl. Combine flours, add to mixture and stir.

Place dough on floured board and knead gently about 10 times to form spongy smooth dough. Flour the rolling pin and roll the dough into an 8-inch square about 1 inch thick. Work the butter with your hands into a neat thin cake and place in the centre of the dough. Fold edges of dough over to cover butter completely. Flatten joint with rolling pin. Then roll pastry to form rectangle (about 18 × 12 inches), being careful not to allow the butter to break through.

Now proceed with the following movement three times: fold dough into thirds; make a half turn so that the open end of the dough is towards you. Roll again into a rectangle. When pastry has been rolled three times, roll once more and cut dough into 3 pieces. Refrigerate 2 while working on the first.

Start with a rectangle and fold in half. Down the open edge cut 2-inch horizontal slits. Open the dough out flat. Spread the surface with equal parts of butter and brown sugar. Spread the cherry pie filling down the middle only. Fold dough over in thirds with the slits on top of filling.

Combine egg and water to make glaze and brush pastry. Preheat oven to 375°F. Let dough rise for ½ hour. Sprinkle with sliced almonds and sugar. Bake in oven until golden, about 12–15 minutes.

Continue the filling, glazing and baking instructions for the remainder of the pastry.

Twice-Baked Hazelnut Cookies

Every country has a version of these nut-rich cookies. They are first baked as a roll and then sliced and baked again. This gives them a toasted flavor which is neither too sweet nor too dry. If you have almonds in the house, they work as well. (Makes 4 dozen cookies)

Ingredients

6	ounces (170 g) shelled hazel-nuts	½	teaspoon vanilla extract
½	cup softened butter	2	cups flour
½	cup sugar	2	teaspoons baking powder
2	eggs	½	teaspoon salt

Method

Preheat oven to 350°F. Spread hazelnuts on a baking sheet and toast in oven 10 minutes. While still warm, rub them together in a tea towel to remove as much of the brown skin as possible. Divide the nuts in half, and grate one-half, leaving the rest whole.

Cream butter and sugar. Beat in eggs and vanilla. Mix together flour, baking powder, salt and grated nuts; add these gradually to the egg mixture, beating well. Then mix in whole nuts.

Form dough into two rolls, each about 16 inches long. Place on a buttered baking sheet and bake at 350°F for 30 minutes, or until lightly golden. Remove from the oven and slice the rolls on the diagonal. Each roll should make about 24 cookies, ½ inch thick. Spread the pieces on a rack over the baking sheet and return to oven. Bake 15 minutes, or until firm and a little more golden. Cool. These keep well in a tightly covered tin.

Rolled Almond Cookies

These butterscotch lacy cookies are crisp and sweet with a nutty after-taste. Leave them flat or even better, roll them around a wooden spoon handle, dip in chocolate and serve as a perky garnish on homemade sherbet or ice cream. (Makes 24 cookies)

Ingredients

½   cup butter
½   cup sugar
2   tablespoons flour
½   teaspoon salt

2   tablespoons 18% or 35% cream
½   cup almonds, blanched and
    finely ground

Method

Preheat oven to 375°F. Prepare baking sheets with parchment paper (or spread with butter and sprinkle with flour). Combine butter, sugar, flour, salt, cream and ground almonds in a saucepan and cook over low heat, stirring until the butter melts and the sugar is dissolved. Continue cooking gently for 3 minutes longer.

Drop teaspoons of mixture on prepared baking sheet, widely spaced apart to give plenty of room for spreading. Bake only 4 at a time for 6–8 minutes or until the cookies are lightly browned around the edges. Watch carefully, and as soon as they are ready, remove from the oven. Allow to cool for a minute or two, then loosen them with a fine spatula and roll round the greased handle of a wooden spoon to make a tube. Slip off carefully and allow to cool. If the cookies cool too quickly and are too brittle to roll, return baking sheet to oven for a moment to soften.

Chocolate Garnish

Melt 4 ounces (100 g) semi-sweet chocolate in the top of a double boiler. When the cookies are cool, dip one end in the chocolate and let it harden.

Food Processor Note: To grind blanched almonds so that they do not become almond butter, add a little sugar during processing.

Holiday Refrigerator Cookies

These colorful and delicate refrigerator cookies are perfect for a busy cook. Prepare them in advance and bake when you need them. They taste like shortbread and look like Christmas. If you want to make them after Christmas is long gone, substitute nuts for the candied peel and red and green cherries. Originally prepared only with flour, we substituted some cornstarch for flour and found that the cookie had a more delicate texture. You'll love them. (Makes 48 1-inch cookies)

Ingredients

¼	cup candied mixed peel	1	teaspoon vanilla
¼	cup red and green cherries, quartered	¾	cup cornstarch
	Boiling water	2	cups all-purpose flour
1	cup unsalted butter	2	tablespoons coarsely chopped walnuts
¾	cup icing sugar, sifted	⅓	cup finely chopped pecans
1	teaspoon grated lemon rind	⅓	cup finely chopped almonds
½	teaspoon salt		

Method

Cover the mixed peel with boiling water, let stand 5 minutes, strain and pat dry. Cover the cherries with boiling water, let stand 5 minutes, strain and pat dry.

Beat the butter until light and fluffy and add sugar, lemon rind, salt and vanilla. Beat for 1 minute. Gradually beat in cornstarch and then beat in the flour until the dough is smooth and well mixed. Divide dough in half. To the first half blend in the cherries and 1 tablespoon of walnuts. Shape into a log 1 inch in diameter and roll the log in chopped almonds. Wrap in waxed paper or plastic wrap and chill for 1 hour.

To the second half of the dough blend in mixed peel and remaining 1 tablespoon of walnuts. Shape into a log 1 inch in diameter and roll the log in chopped pecans. Wrap in waxed paper or plastic wrap and chill for 1 hour.

Preheat oven to 375°F. Cut the chilled logs into ¼-inch slices. Bake on a lightly greased or parchment covered cookie sheet, for 12–15 minutes.

These cookies may be varied by adding only nuts or cherries, or rolling in chopped walnuts or chocolate bits. Your imagination is the only limit to their variety.

FRUIT DESSERTS

Pierre's Favorite Lemon Jelly *123*
Lemon and Strawberry Sherbet *123*
Cold Lime Soufflé *124*
Apricot Yogurt Dessert *126*
Rhubarb Custard *125*
Winter Fruit Salad *126*
Fruit Mousse with Hazelnuts *125*

BAKED FRUIT DESSERTS

Apple Strudel *128*
Cream Cheese Tartlet Shells *127*
Apple Tart with Cinnamon *130*
Apple Tart Maison Basque *130*
Applesauce Apple Flan *129*
Lemon Flan *134*
Armagnac Prune Soufflé *131*
Crêpes Soufflé Roxelane *132*
Cherry Soufflé Pudding *133*
Omelette Soufflé *134*
Steamed Pear-Cranberry Pudding *135*
Fig Pudding *136*
Bonnie Stern's Lemon Cheesecake *137*

CHOCOLATE DESSERTS

Bonnie Stern's Chocolate Cheesecake *138*
Chocolate Chip Meringue Cake *138*
Tiramisu' *141*
Chocolate Soufflé *140*
Chocolate Applesauce Cake *139*

CREAM DESSERTS and SAUCES

Cream Cheese Hearts with Fruit *142*
Floating Islands *142*
Butter Sauce *143*
Sabayon Sauce with Marsala *143*

Pierre's Favorite Lemon Jelly

Janet Berton let us in on her secret—this is Pierre's favorite dessert! (Serves 6)

Ingredients

2	¼-ounce packages (7 g) unflavored gelatin	1	cup freshly squeezed lemon juice
½	cup cold water	12–15	ice cubes
1½	cups boiling water	1	tablespoon grated lemon rind
½–¾	cup sugar		

Method

In a large 4-cup glass measuring cup soak the gelatin in the cold water (add gelatin to the water). Add the boiling water, stirring to completely dissolve the gelatin. Add the sugar and stir well. Add lemon juice.

Add enough ice cubes to fill the measuring cup to the 4-cup level. Stir until the jelly begins to thicken. Remove any remaining ice cubes. Add lemon rind and pour into a mold or allow to set in the refrigerator in the cup and, when chilled, place into individual dishes.

Lemon and Strawberry Sherbet

Sherbet is refreshing and surprisingly simple to make. Its natural flavor leaves you feeling marvelously refreshed. (Serves 6)

Ingredients

1	cup water	½	teaspoon grated lemon rind
1	cup sugar	1	11-ounce package (300 g) frozen unsweetened straw-berries, thawed, drained and mashed
	Pinch salt		
½	cup light (10%) cream		
½	cup lemon juice	2	egg whites

Method

Place water, ¾ cup sugar and salt in a saucepan and bring to a boil. Boil for 5 minutes. Cool completely in the refrigerator. Stir in cream, lemon juice and rind. Pour into metal ice cube tray and freeze until firm.

Turn mixture into a bowl, add mashed strawberries and beat until smooth. Beat the egg whites until soft peaks form. Gradually beat in remaining ¼ cup sugar until mixture is stiff and glossy. Fold into lemon-strawberry mixture and freeze until firm. Remove and whip again. Freeze. Serve.

Cold Lime Soufflé

Here is one of Bonnie Stern's beautiful desserts. She made it in a cut glass bowl and garnished it with turns of sliced lime. If you wish to make it without the whipping cream, increase the number of eggs to six. (Serves 6–8)

Ingredients

1	envelope (7 g) unflavored gelatin	⅔	cup fresh lime juice
			Zest of 2 limes, finely grated
¼	cup cold water	¼	teaspoon cream of tartar
4	eggs, separated	1¾	cups whipping cream
¾	cup sugar		

Garnish

	A little whipped cream from above	1	tablespoon rum
			Grated coconut, toasted
1	tablespoon icing sugar	1	lime, thinly sliced

Method

Sprinkle gelatin over cold water in a saucepan and allow to soften. Beat ½ cup sugar with egg yolks until mixture is light and lemony. Beat in lime juice and zest.

Heat gelatin mixture gently until gelatin dissolves. Beat into egg yolk mixture and return everything to the saucepan. Cook very gently, stirring constantly, until mixture becomes slightly custardy. Transfer to a large bowl and cool until syrupy but not lumpy. (If mixture has curdled at all while cooking simply strain it before cooling.)

Beat egg whites with cream of tartar (or 1 teaspoon lemon juice) until light. Add remaining ¼ cup sugar one tablespoon at a time and beat very well after each addition. Continue beating until egg whites are very stiff and sugar has dissolved.

Beat whipping cream until light but not too stiff. Stir ⅓ of the egg whites into the gelatin mixture. Fold in the remaining whites and most of the cream (reserve about ½ cup for the garnish). Pour mixture into individual serving dishes, a large serving bowl or a soufflé dish fitted with a collar and refrigerate at least 3 hours before serving.

Meanwhile add icing sugar and rum to remaining cream and beat until stiff. Pipe or spoon cream decoratively on the top of soufflé and garnish with toasted coconut and lime slices. *Note:* In summer fresh raspberries or blueberries make a beautiful garnish for this dessert.

Rhubarb Custard

Imagine a combination of tart rhubarb and creamy sweet custard. Then, try making it. I hope you like it as much as we do. (Serves 4–6)

Ingredients

2	pounds (1 kg) rhubarb, washed and cut into 1-inch pieces	3	egg yolks
¼	cup sugar	3	tablespoons sugar
1	teaspoon ground ginger	1	teaspoon cornstarch
1	cup whipping cream	1	teaspoon vanilla

Method

Cook rhubarb, ¼ cup sugar and ginger together over medium heat for about 10 minutes until the rhubarb is tender. Drain.

Heat whipping cream. Mix egg yolks, 3 tablespoons sugar, cornstarch and vanilla together until smooth. Whisk warm whipping cream into egg yolk mixture slowly. Return to saucepan. Heat until thickened over medium heat about 5 minutes. Pour into bowl and cool.

To serve swirl rhubarb and custard together in sherbet glasses or put rhubarb into sherbet glasses and top with custard.

Fruit Mousse with Hazelnuts

While Executive Chef Niels Kjeldson lists peaches, plums, apples, pears and other fruits in this recipe, I have used different combinations with complete success. Prepare the fruits, reduce the syrup and whip the cream ahead of time; just before serving, whip the egg whites and combine all of the ingredients together. (Serves 2)

Ingredients

1	peach, skin removed	½	orange
1	plum	2	egg whites, beaten until stiff
½	pear	¼	cup whipping cream, beaten
½	apple	1	tablespoon toasted, sliced hazelnuts
4	strawberries		
4	cherries		

Method

Cut all fruit into small pieces and purée in a blender. Place in a fine strainer over a bowl and let drain for 10 minutes. Boil the juice until it becomes thick, then add it to the fruit pulp. Fold in the egg whites, the whipping cream and toasted sliced hazelnuts. Pour into champagne glasses and chill 2 hours.

Apricot Yogurt Dessert

Shirley Conran, who tested this dessert with me last winter prefers it frozen. I don't as it is too cold. Either way, it is light and tangy. (Serves 8)

Ingredients

1	package (250 g) dried apricots	4	tablespoons water
3	tablespoons apricot brandy or apple juice	1¼	cups yogurt
1	cup crushed crumbs (Graham cracker, vanilla wafer or short-bread cookie)	1	cup whipping cream, whipped until stiff
¼	cup melted butter	1	tablespoon lemon juice
½	teaspoon cinnamon	⅓	cup sugar
1	package (7 g) unflavored gelatin		Toasted almonds

Method

Scissor all but 8 apricots into strips. Save these for garnish. Soak the slices in brandy or juice for 2 hours.

Combine crumbs, melted butter and cinnamon. Mix well. Press into bottom of a large 9-inch spring form pan. Set aside. Dissolve gelatin in water over low heat and cool. Blend yogurt, whipped cream, lemon juice and sugar. Stir in dissolved gelatin and drained apricots. Pour into crumb crust and refrigerate until set.

Garnish with the 8 whole apricots and toasted slivered almonds.

Winter Fruit Salad

Whenever I'm asked to bring a dessert for a party, picnic or bazaar, I think of this. It tastes divine, looks even better and doesn't spill in the car on the way. I serve it in an attractive cut glass bowl. Moreover, in winter it has that real fruit taste we so desire. (Serves 4)

Ingredients

4	figs, dried	2	oranges
6	pitted prunes, dried	1	large apple
4	peach halves, dried	1	large pear
8	apricot halves, dried	2	bananas
1	lemon	¼	cup sugar

Method

Steam dried fruits over boiling water until softened, 10–20 minutes. Grate the lemon rind and half the rind of one of the oranges. Put them in a large bowl and squeeze the lemon juice into the bowl.

Peel the remaining 1½ oranges and remove all the white pith. Cut into ½-inch slices then cut each slice into quarters, reserving the juice. Remove any seeds, then add the oranges and their juice to the bowl.

Peel and core the apple and pear and cut into bite-size pieces. Add them to the bowl and stir, coating them with lemon juice to prevent discoloration. Slice in the bananas and stir.

Cut the dried fruits into small pieces and add them to the bowl. Sprinkle the sugar over the fruit and mix gently but thoroughly. Cover and chill for several hours before serving.

Cream Cheese Tartlet Shells

This quick, rich pastry is extraordinary. Try our Lemon Curd (see p. 148) in these tarts for special occasions. (Makes 60 small tart shells)

Ingredients

1	cup butter, at room temperature	1	package (225 g) cream cheese, at room temperature
		2	cups all-purpose flour

Method

Beat the butter and cream cheese in a large bowl until light and fluffy. Add the flour and stir until the mixture forms a ball. Wrap in plastic wrap and chill for an hour. Take off a small part of the dough, keeping the rest in the refrigerator, and roll out on a lightly floured board until thin, about ⅛ inch thick. Cut the dough with floured, round cutters and press them gently into ungreased small tartlet cups. Press the dough evenly against the sides of the cups. Fill with desired filling and bake. If you are preparing the tart shells in advance, keep them refrigerated. Bake in a preheated 350°F oven for 20–25 minutes. Cool on a wire rack and serve at room temperature.

Food Processor Method

Place the flour in the work bowl which has been fitted with the steel blade. The butter and cheese should be very cold. Place them in the freezer for a few minutes before using. Cut into 1-inch squares and drop down the feed tube with the motor running. The dough should form a ball at this stage; if not, add 2 tablespoons of ice water with the motor running. Wrap in plastic wrap and refrigerate. Continue as you would with the conventional method.

Apple Strudel

Gay Cook, whose cooking school has attracted followers from all over Canada, demonstrated her strudel with awesome skill. Even she had some tears in the dough, which made the rest of us feel quite comfortable with our imperfections. Many viewers wrote to tell us of their success after watching Gay. (Serves 8)

Ingredients

Dough

1	cup all-purpose flour—not blended flour	½	egg (1½ tablespoons blended yolk and white)
¼	teaspoon salt	1	tablespoon melted lard or 2 tablespoons melted butter
3	tablespoons lukewarm water		

Method

With Food Processor or Kitchen Machine

Place flour and salt in mixer with dough hook or in food processor with steel blade. Combine the egg, water and melted lard or butter. With kitchen machine running, add the combined liquid and beat to mix until dough leaves sides of mixer bowl, or if using processor, until dough forms a mass. Feel dough. It should be slightly sticky but soft. Continue beating or processing for another minute. Remove dough from machine and smooth it into a ball, knead for several minutes by slapping it against the surface of the table.

Hand Method

Place flour on pastry board, making a large well in the centre. Combine the liquids in the well with the salt. Using a fork, start to gradually mix the flour into the liquids, then finish mixing with your fingers, slapping the surface of the board with the dough.

Allow the dough to rest for 45 minutes on the board, with warm metal or porcelain bowl placed over it.

Ingredients

Filling

1¼	pounds (600-700 g) firm apples—McIntosh, Northern Spy, Granny Smith	⅓	cup coarsely chopped almonds (optional)
½	cup sugar	1	teaspoon cinnamon
⅓	cup raisins or currants	⅓	cup melted butter

Method

Quarter, peel, core the apples, then slice thinly. Combine the rest of the ingredients except the butter in a bowl with the apples. Spread a clean sheet or table cloth over a table. Sprinkle lightly with flour. Place dough in centre of sheet and roll into a circle about 12 inches in diameter. To stretch dough, lift it and drape over lightly floured hands. Gently stretch dough from the centre rotating the entire mass as you work. Then place it on the cloth, reach under and gently stretch the dough one small area after another, until paper thin and measuring at least 30 inches in diameter. If possible let dough hang over the edge of the table.

Cut off the thick edge with scissors and discard that dough or use for noodles. Brush the dough surface with some of the melted butter. Sprinkle the apple mixture over the dough. Fold in the sides, then by lifting the sheet, roll up the strudel, not too tightly, brushing the dough with butter as you turn.

Slip the strudel onto a buttered baking sheet with sides. Prick the top with a sharp knife tip several times.

Bake in 450°F oven for 10 minutes, then reduce oven heat to 400°F for another 20–30 minutes. During the baking, baste the strudel with the juices that form on the pan using a brush. This helps to glaze the strudel dough. When strudel is golden brown, remove from the oven and dust with powdered sugar. Serve in slices while still warm.

Applesauce Apple Flan

If you prefer your apple flan without custard, use applesauce as a base. It makes a nice change. (Serves 4–6)

Ingredients

	Pastry for a 9-inch pie plate	4 or 5	large tart apples
2	cups thick applesauce, spiced	½	cup apricot jam
		¼	cup water

Method

Preheat oven to 425°F. Roll the pastry and fit into a pie plate, preferably one with straight sides and fluted edges. Spoon applesauce over bottom. Pare and core the apples and slice them thinly. Arrange slices on applesauce in concentric circles. Combine the apricot jam and water, heat and stir until the mixture is well blended. Spread over apple slices. Bake for about 30 minutes or until apples are tender.

Apple Tart Maison Basque

From the Basque region of southern France, a recipe from chef Roger Dufau. It's different from Chef Sonszogni's tart because the apples are cooked and served under a crisp meringue topping. (Serves 4)

Ingredients

6	apples, peeled, cored and sliced	2	egg yolks, beaten
3	tablespoons sugar	1	9-inch pie shell, unbaked
2	tablespoons butter	2	egg whites
	Grated rind of 1 lemon	1	tablespoon sugar

Method

Combine apples, sugar, butter and grated lemon rind together in a saucepan. Simmer slowly, stirring occasionally until mixture is reduced to pulp. Beat well until smooth, then add beaten egg yolks and blend well. Pour mixture into prepared pie shell. Bake in 375°F oven for 30 minutes or until mixture is firm and the pastry is done.

Whisk egg whites until stiff, sprinkle with sugar and pile meringue on top. Return to 325°F oven until golden brown and set, about 10–15 minutes.

Apple Tart with Cinnamon

Herbert Sonszogni's famous apple tart is so simple: its mystery probably lies in the fact that it has never been recorded. Make a quick crust in the food processor. Herbert recommends using a flan pan with a removable bottom. For variation add some ground hazelnuts to the crust. (Serves 8)

Ingredients

	Sweet pastry to line a 10-inch flan pan (see *What's Cooking*, Vol. 1, p. 120)	1	teaspoon cinnamon
		2	eggs
		¾	cup 18% cream
4	large apples, peeled and cut into eighths	1	tablespoon sugar
		1	teaspoon vanilla
1	teaspoon sugar		Icing sugar

Method

Preheat oven to 350°F. Line the flan pan with the sweet pastry. Mix the apples with sugar and cinnamon in a stainless steel bowl. Fill the pan and bake for 20 minutes. The apples are ready if they are soft when pricked with a fork and the crust edges turn slightly brown.

Whisk the custard ingredients, eggs, cream, sugar and vanilla, and pour mixture over the apples. Bake another 20 minutes. Remove from the oven and dust with icing sugar. Serve with whipped cream.

Armagnac Prune Soufflé

For those who think that prunes are dull fare, here's a light unusual soufflé that lifts them into the party class. The imaginative combination of prunes and Armagnac is unexpected and well worth trying. Diane Dexter of San Francisco shared this recipe with me and now I share it happily with you. It's delicious served with Roquefort or Gorgonzola. Try it. (Serves 6)

Ingredients

Purée

1	pound (500 g) dried prunes	½	teaspoon vanilla
½	lemon rind, thinly pared	3	tablespoons Armagnac
1	cup water		Pinch of salt
1	cup white wine	1–2	tablespoons cream
3	egg yolks	1–2	tablespoons sugar

Meringue

5	egg whites		Pinch of cream of tartar
	Pinch of salt	4	tablespoons sugar

Method

Wash the prunes and soak overnight in cold water. Prepare the purée by simmering the fruit and lemon rind in the water and white wine until the prunes are soft and swollen. Meanwhile, preheat oven to 400°F. Butter a 6-cup soufflé pan or 6 individual soufflé cups and sprinkle with sugar.

Drain and stone the prunes. Purée in a blender or work through a sieve adding enough water to make a mixture the consistency of thick applesauce: a spoon should stand in it. You should have about 1 cup of purée.

Beat the yolks, vanilla, Armagnac, salt and cream into the prune purée. Taste and add sugar if necessary—it should be moderately sweet. Cover and keep warm.

Beat the egg whites with a pinch of salt and cream of tartar and beat in the sugar, one tablespoon at a time. When stiffened, fold into the prune mixture in thirds and spoon into soufflé dishes. Individual dishes will take 10–15 minutes, a large dish will take 35–40 minutes. Serve immediately.

Variations: Use dried apricots or pears instead of the prunes with Poire William or Cointreau.

Sprinkle in crushed Amaretti cookies, macaroons or praline as you fold in the egg whites.

Fresh diced berries may be added. Fresh raspberries or boysenberries are specially delicious folded in with the egg whites.

Crêpes Soufflé Roxelane

Here is another delicious dessert from Diane Dexter. This is a soufflé baked in individual crêpes. Crisp on the outside, light and soft in the centre—and flavored with Cointreau! The crêpes can be made ahead of time and frozen so that there won't be so much to do on the dinner evening. It takes a while but it's worth the trouble; however, a word to the wise—serve immediately from the oven with rich Melba sauce. An absolute winner. (12–14 soufflé crêpes)

Ingredients

12–14 crêpes, 8-inches in diameter

Soufflé mixture

1	cup milk	4	tablespoons Cointreau
3	tablespoons flour		Pinch of salt
5	tablespoons sugar		Lemon juice to taste
5	eggs, separated and at room temperature		Melted butter
	Grated zest of 2 lemons		Confectioner's sugar to decorate

Sauce

2	cups frozen unsweetened raspberries	3	tablespoons sugar
2	tablespoons red currant jelly		Cointreau to taste

Method

Mix together the milk, flour and 1 tablespoon sugar. Cook over low heat until mixture simmers and thickens. Leave to cool, stirring after 4–5 minutes. Beat 3 of the yolks and add them. Place over low heat stirring constantly until the mixture barely bubbles. Remove from the heat and add the grated lemon zest, remaining 2 egg yolks and the Cointreau. Add lemon juice and salt to taste.

Beat the egg whites to soft peaks and stir in the remaining 4 tablespoons sugar to stiffen them slightly. Carefully fold into the lemon mixture in 4 batches.

Preheat oven to 400°F. Spread each crêpe with a little melted butter using a brush. Spoon about 4 tablespoons of soufflé mixture onto each crêpe taking it right out to the edge so crêpe won't seal. Fold in half or roll loosely. Place on a buttered baking sheet and bake for about 10 minutes. (You may have to test one to get the exact baking time.) Sprinkle with confectioner's sugar and serve immediately with Melba Sauce.

Melba Sauce

Purée and strain the raspberries. Add red currant jelly, sugar and Cointreau to taste.

Cherry Soufflé Pudding

If your family had hot puddings for dessert on cold winter days long ago, this cheery cherry soufflé will bring a rush of memories flooding back. (Serves 6)

Ingredients

2   cups pitted cherries

Syrup

1	cup water	$\frac{1}{2}$	cup butter, softened
1	cup white wine	$\frac{2}{3}$	cup sugar
$\frac{1}{2}$	cup sugar	6	eggs, separated
	Lemon slice		Few drops of vanilla
	Pinch of cinnamon		Pinch of cinnamon
		$1\frac{1}{4}$	cups dry breadcrumbs

Sauce

$\frac{1}{4}$	cup Port or Madeira	3	tablespoons sweet butter

Method

Prepare soufflé pan by buttering and dusting with breadcrumbs. In a saucepan combine water, wine, sugar, lemon slice and cinnamon. Halve the cherries and poach gently in the syrup until soft. Drain and cool, reserving the poaching liquid.

Preheat oven to 375°F. Cream the butter and sugar. Beat the egg yolks and add one at a time, then the vanilla and cinnamon. Stir in the breadcrumbs and then the poached cherries. Beat the egg whites to soft peaks and fold into the mixture in thirds. Turn into soufflé pan and bake for 35–40 minutes or until well puffed and lightly browned.

Serve warm from the pan with a sauce made by reducing the poaching liquid with the Port or Madeira to a syrupy consistency. At the last moment swirl in the sweet butter. This dessert is also delicious served with softly whipped cream.

Omelette Soufflé

Irena Chalmers demonstrated this creamy, moist dessert soufflé—we couldn't decide whether it was more of a soufflé than an omelette or vice versa, but we all decided it was a winner! For higher volume, keep the eggs at room temperature for a while before whipping. (Serves 8)

Ingredients

1	tablespoon butter	12	egg whites
9	egg yolks	1/8	teaspoon salt
3/4	cup sugar	1/4	teaspoon cream of tartar (optional)
1/4	cup spirits (Grand Marnier, Amaretto, rum, kirsch, Kahlua, Cognac, Framboise)	2	teaspoons powdered sugar for decoration
1	teaspoon vanilla extract		

Method

Preheat the oven to 375°F. Grease a 2 inch × 10 inch × 17 inch oval au gratin pan or any attractive 2–2½-quart shallow baking dish with 1 tablespoon butter. Beat the egg yolks for about a minute with an electric mixer or a whisk. Gradually add the sugar. When the mixture is thick, add the spirits and the vanilla. Beat about 30 seconds to incorporate.

Beat the egg whites with salt and the optional cream of tartar until they form stiff, moist peaks. Fold 1 cup of the whites into the yolk mixture to lighten it. Then, using a large whisk, fold the yolks into the remaining whites until the entire mixture is incorporated and a pale yellow color.

In the buttered au gratin pan, heap the mixture in an oval-shaped mound about 4 inches high. Smooth the mixture with a spoon. Then, make an indentation lengthwise about 1 inch deep into the uncooked mixture. Bake for 20 minutes until the soufflé is well puffed and browned. Use a sieve to dust with powdered sugar, if you wish. Serve the soufflé immediately.

Lemon Flan

Maison Basque's famous Tarte aux Citron. (Makes 2 flans)

Ingredients

	Pastry to line 2 10-inch flan pans		Grated lemon rind of 4 lemons
1	cup butter, softened	6	eggs
1	cup 35% cream	1	cup sugar
1	cup fresh lemon juice (use 10-12 lemons)		

Method

Preheat oven to 325°F. Mix together the softened butter, cream, lemon juice and grated lemon rind until smooth. Beat eggs with fork or wire whisk until yolks and whites are well mixed. Add sugar and blend. Add egg mixture to the lemon mixture and blend. Divide in half and spoon mixture into pastry shells. Bake for about 30 minutes or until golden brown.

Steamed Pear-Cranberry Pudding

A steamed pudding with less calories than the traditional ones. No less delicious, though. For even fewer calories, leave the butter sauce off the table. (Makes 6–8 servings)

Ingredients

1	14-ounce (398 mL) can pears (no sugar added)	2	teaspoons baking soda
1	cup halved cranberries	½	teaspoon salt
1½	cup all-purpose flour	½	cup molasses

Method

Drain pear juice and heat ½ cup to boiling point. Dice pears and combine with cranberries. In medium-sized bowl combine flour, soda and salt. Add fruit and mix well. Combine hot pear juice with molasses and stir into mixture. Pour into greased 1½ quart (1.5 L) mold, filling only ⅔ full to allow for expansion during cooking. Cover with lid or greased foil. Place on rack in deep kettle. Add boiling water to come halfway up side of mold. Cover and let simmer for 2 hours or until toothpick inserted in centre comes out clean. Cool mold on wire rack for 10 minutes. Loosen pudding and invert onto serving plate. Serve warm or cold with Butter Sauce (see p. 143).

Microwave Instructions

Prepare the pudding as the recipe directs, then pour the batter into a 1½ quart (1.5 L) glass or microwave plastic ring mold. It should be only two-thirds full. Cover loosely with plastic wrap, elevate and bake 12–16 minutes on Medium (50% Power). Rotate pan during cooking if necessary. Test with a toothpick inserted in the centre—it should come out clean.

Fig Pudding

Serve this delightful pudding with a rum hard sauce or plain butter sauce at holiday time. (Serves 10)

Ingredients

1	pound (500 g) figs, stemmed and chopped	¾	teaspoon salt
1¾	cups milk	¾	pound (375 g) ground suet
1½	cups all-purpose flour	1	cup sugar
2½	teaspoons baking powder	3	eggs
1	teaspoon ground nutmeg	1½	cups fresh breadcrumbs
1	teaspoon ground cinnamon	3	tablespoons grated orange rind

Method

Rinse a heavy saucepan with cold water then combine figs and milk in it and bring milk just to the boiling point over very low heat, simmer the mixture, stirring for 20 minutes. Let it cool.

Meanwhile, combine flour, baking powder, nutmeg, cinnamon and salt. In a large bowl, cream suet with sugar until fluffy, then add eggs, one at a time, beating well after each addition. Stir in breadcrumbs and orange rind. Add flour mixture alternately with fig mixture, beating well. Pour into a 2-quart (2 L) pudding mold, cover with lid or greased foil. Put mold on rack in deep kettle. Add boiling water to come halfway up sides of mold. Steam, covered for 2 hours, until toothpick comes out clean. Remove and let cool, covered for 20 minutes. Remove lid, invert onto plate and serve warm.

Microwave Instructions

Combine figs and milk in a 1½-quart glass casserole. Cover and cook for 4 minutes on Full Power. Stir and cook for 8–10 minutes on Medium (50% Power), until very soft. Let cool.

Follow the recipe directions, pouring batter in glass or microwave plastic 2-quart (2 L) ring mold. Cover with plastic wrap, elevate in the centre of the microwave on custard cups, inverted saucers or microwave roasting rack.

Bake 14–18 minutes on Medium (50% Power) or until a toothpick inserted in the centre comes out clean. Rotate the dish if necessary during cooking.

Bonnie Stern's Lemon Cheesecake

(Serves 6–8)

Ingredients

2	tablespoons unsalted butter, softened	4	eggs
			Finely grated peel of 1 lemon
⅓	cup almonds or hazelnuts, toasted and finely chopped		Juice of 1 lemon (¼ cup)
		1	teaspoon pure vanilla extract
4	packages (225 g each) Philadelphia cream cheese	12	strawberries
		2	kiwi fruit
1½	cups sugar	¼	cup raspberry jelly

Method

Preheat oven to 350°F. Butter an 8-inch cheesecake pan or an 8-inch springform pan and sprinkle bottom and sides with nuts. If you are using a springform pan, wrap pan with tin foil to prevent bottom of pan from leaking.

Beat cheese until very smooth. Beat in sugar gradually. Add eggs one at a time but do not overbeat once eggs have been added. Beat in lemon peel, juice and vanilla. Pour batter into prepared pan and level the top. Place pan in a large pan of hot water (to come partly up the sides of the cheesecake pan) and place in the oven. Bake 1–1¼ hours. When cake is ready it should be slightly puffed, barely turning brown and still slightly loose in the centre. Remove from water bath and cool on wire rack. Run a knife around edge of cake.

When cake has reached room temperature, invert cake onto a cake plate.

Peel kiwi fruit and slice very thinly crosswise. Hull strawberries and slice in half. Decorate the top of the cake (actually upside-down bottom) with kiwis and strawberries. Brush lightly with the jelly to prevent drying. Refrigerate until ready to serve, at least 6 hours. This cake freezes well, but freeze before decorating with fruit.

Bonnie Stern's Chocolate Cheesecake

Serve with whipped cream flavored with Cognac, rum or orange liqueur. (Serves 12)

Ingredients

Crust

1	cup chocolate wafer cookies, ground	½	cup hazelnuts, finely chopped
		⅓	cup butter, melted

Filling

12	squares (28 g each) semisweet chocolate	3	eggs
			Pinch of salt
1½	pounds (675 g) cream cheese	1	teaspoon pure vanilla extract
1	cup sugar	1	cup sour cream

Glaze

4	squares (28 g each) semisweet chocolate	2–4	tablespoons heavy (whipping) cream

Method

Preheat oven to 350°F. Butter a 9- or 10-inch springform pan. Combine chocolate wafers, nuts and butter. Blend well. Pat most of the mixture into the bottom of the pan but pat a little up the sides too. Set aside.

Melt chocolate in the top of a double boiler over gently simmering water. Remove from the heat and cool slightly.

Beat cheese until very light and gradually beat in the sugar. Mix in chocolate and the eggs one at a time. Add salt, vanilla and sour cream, stirring until just blended and smooth.

Spoon mixture into prepared pan and bake 50–60 minutes. Do not worry if top cracks slightly. Cake may seem soft but will firm up when cold. Cool to room temperature and then refrigerate overnight.

For the glaze, melt the chocolate with the cream and stir until smooth. Spread over top of cake and allow to set. Remove cake from pan by running a knife around the inside edge of pan and loosening the sides.

Chocolate Chip Meringue Cake

Dufflet, Toronto's diminutive queen of the cakes provides this recipe for chocolate meringue cake. Isn't it wonderful?

Ingredients

Meringue

6	egg whites	2	tablespoons cocoa powder
1	cup sugar	½	cup semisweet chocolate chips

Buttercream

6 ounces melted semisweet chocolate	½ pound unsalted butter
	2 eggs

Method

Preheat oven to 225°F. Line 3 cookie sheets with parchment paper. Draw 3 9-inch circles with pencil. Whip egg whites in large mixing bowl until very soft peaks form. Gradually whip in ⅔ cup of the sugar. Continue whipping until stiff peaks form. Sift together remaining sugar and cocoa. Fold into egg whites with chocolate chips.

Fill large piping bag with the meringue mixture. With #8 plain tip pipe in continuous circles filling the 3 circles.

Bake for 1½-2 hours, until meringues feel light and dry to the touch.

Melt chocolate for buttercream. Cool. Whip butter until fluffy. Add chocolate and continue whipping. Add eggs one at a time. Continue until buttercream is very light.

Place one meringue on serving platter and ice with buttercream. Place another layer overtop and ice. Add remaining layer and ice sides and top. Decorate top with chocolate shavings or curls.

Chocolate Applesauce Cake

Ingredients

⅔ cup raisins	¾ cup butter
1½ cups all-purpose flour	1½ cups sugar
2 teaspoons baking soda	3 eggs
¼ teaspoon salt	2 cups applesauce
2 teaspoons cinnamon	½ cup chopped walnuts
¼ teaspoon nutmeg	Icing sugar
5 tablespoons cocoa	

Method

Preheat oven to 350°F. Grease a 10-inch tube pan. Cover raisins with boiling water. Let stand 5 minutes, drain. Combine flour, baking soda, salt, cinnamon, nutmeg and cocoa. In large bowl, cream butter and sugar and beat well. Add eggs, one at a time, beating thoroughly after each addition. Add dry ingredients, alternately with applesauce, ending with dry ingredients. Stir in raisins and nuts. Turn into prepared pan and bake 1 hour. Cool in pan. Remove cake and when completely cooled, sprinkle with icing sugar.

Chocolate Soufflé

New York City holds perhaps more chocoholics than all of Canada and so, when I want the best chocolate recipes, I go there. Here's one, from chocolate specialist Nan Mabon. (Serves 8)

Ingredients

¼	cup softened butter	10	egg whites
⅓	cup flour	⅓	cup sugar
1½	cups milk	1	tablespoon cocoa powder
6	squares semisweet chocolate	½	teaspoon cream of tartar
6	egg yolks		

Method

Prepare 2-quart (2 L) soufflé dish by buttering the inside of it with some softened butter, sprinkle with sugar and shake out excess. Measure a piece of foil for a collar, butter the inside and place around the dish, then secure with string.

Press the butter and flour together with your fingers or a fork. Heat the milk in a pan and slowly add the butter-flour mixture, whisking until smooth. Continue to cook over medium heat until thickened. Remove from heat. Let cool.

Melt 4 squares of chocolate in the top of a double boiler. Stir the yolks into the chocolate, off the heat, then add the milk mixture, stirring until well blended. Cool. Preheat the oven to 350°F. Grate the remaining 2 squares of chocolate and set aside.

Whip the whites in a very large bowl until foamy and lightly thickened then slowly add the sugar, cocoa powder and cream of tartar, continuing to whip until stiff but not dry.

Stir one heaping tablespoon of the whites into the completely cooled chocolate base, then place ⅓ of the base mixture on top of the whites, fold and repeat until the two are blended. Do this very carefully so that you don't deflate the air you have so carefully beaten into the whites. Pour half into the prepared dish then sprinkle the grated 2 squares of chocolate on top. Cover with the remaining soufflé mixture.

Place the dish carefully in the middle rack of the preheated oven and bake 55–60 minutes. Serve immediately.

A soufflé will usually hold in the oven for about 10 minutes (with the heat turned off). Serve with 1 cup of lightly whipped, sweetened heavy cream.

Tiramisu'

Here's a chocolate dessert from the land of pasta. Guiliano Bugialli serves this in Florence when the dinner is light and lasts several hours into the night. (Serves 6)

Ingredients

2	cups strong espresso coffee	6	tablespoons granulated sugar
4	squares (28 g each) bitter chocolate	1	pound (500 g) non-commercial creamed cottage or cream cheese (sold in bulk only at cheese shops)
24	lady fingers		
6	eggs separated		
1	teaspoon cream of tartar		

Method

Prepare a very strong espresso coffee and let cool completely. Coarsely chop the chocolate or cut it into small pieces. Lightly soak the lady fingers with the cold coffee and arrange half of them in one layer on a serving dish with high sides.

With a wooden spoon, mix the egg yolks together with the sugar. Beat the cheese to soften it and add to the yolks. Stir gently to mix. Beat the egg whites until stiff, adding the cream of tartar after the first 30 seconds of beating. Gently fold the stiff egg whites into the cheese-yolk mixture.

Make a layer with half of this mixture on top of the lady fingers, sprinkle with some grated chocolate, then repeat procedure to make another layer of soaked lady fingers, cheese-yolk mixture and chocolate.

Place serving dish in the refrigerator for at least 1 hour before serving.

Floating Islands

This simple old-time dessert rivals caramel custard for popularity in the chic restaurants of Toronto. Serve them at a candlelit dinner and soak in the praise. (Serves 6)

Ingredients

1½ cups milk	1½ teaspoons vanilla
3 egg yolks	3 egg whites
⅓ cup sugar	¼ cup sugar
Pinch of salt	

Method

Scald milk in top of double boiler. Beat egg yolks with sugar and salt until well blended. Gradually whisk hot milk into egg mixture, beating constantly. Return mixture to double boiler over hot, not boiling water. Cook, stirring constantly until custard coats a metal spoon, about 10 minutes. Pour into individual baking dishes (custard cups) or a 1-quart baking dish.

Beat egg whites until soft peaks form. Gradually add the ¼ cup sugar, continue beating until stiff peaks form. Float spoonfuls of meringue on each custard. Broil 2 minutes or until tips of meringue are golden brown.

Cream Cheese Hearts with Fruit

This dessert is usually made with rich cream, enriched further with cream cheese and sour cream. This version uses yogurt and the result is incredibly light, airy and delicious. I like individual servings because they look so pretty on the plate; however if the heart-shaped molds are unavailable, use a plain sieve. They taste wonderful with a side dish of stewed figs. In the summer a tablespoon of fresh raspberries and blueberries overtop is gorgeous. (Serves 6)

Ingredients

¾ cup 35% cream	4 egg whites
¾ cup plain yogurt	

Method

Prepare six white-glazed, hole-pierced heart molds by lining each with a large square of cheesecloth, muslin or a well-rinsed J-cloth. Or simply use a large sieve. Whip cream until stiff, beat yogurt smooth and fold into cream; beat egg whites to soft peaks and fold all together.

Spoon mixture into each mold until slightly too full; rap molds on table to settle contents, fold over each cloth to cover cream, and place molds on flat plates in refrigerator or larder to drain overnight. The cream will set into heart shapes.

To serve, carefully fold back cloths and invert each mold onto the centre of a dessert plate. Lift off mold, gently detach cloth, smooth any ragged edges, and serve with sliced stewed figs or raspberries and strawberries.

Sabayon Sauce with Marsala

When a simple dessert of fresh fruit is not elegant enough, ready all of these ingredients beside a steaming double boiler and whip up just before serving. Pour the luscious sauce over fruits such as kiwi, strawberries or pineapple. (Serves 4)

Ingredients

3	egg yolks	¼	cup Marsala wine
1	whole egg	¼	cup dry white wine
3	tablespoons sugar		Dash of lemon juice

Method

Mix together all ingredients and heat until thick and frothy over double boiler. Remove from the heat. Serve with fresh fruit.

Butter Sauce

(Makes 1 cup)

Ingredients

6	tablespoons unsalted butter	6	tablespoons half and half cream
¾	cup sugar		

Method

Combine butter, sugar and half and half cream in small saucepan. Cook and stir until sugar is dissolved.

Microwave Instructions

Combine the ingredients in a 2-cup glass measure. Cook, uncovered for 2–3 minutes on Full Power until the sugar is dissolved.

Et Cetera

Fancy Oils and Vinegars 145
Harvey Kirck's Barbecue Sauce 145
Barbecue Sauce 146
Chinese 5-Spice Powder 146
Cranberry Ketchup 147
Homemade Horseradish 146
Horseradish Sauce 149
Mint Sauce 148
Banana Ginger Chutney 149
Pear, Apple & Nut Chutney 150
Lemon Curd 148
Lemon Marmalade 148

Fancy Oils and Vinegars

Dinah Koo, a regular visitor to "What's Cooking," runs Dinah's Cupboard in downtown Toronto. She imports the latest and newest of foodstuffs. She suggests some interesting ideas for dressing up ordinary foods with fancy oils and vinegars; for instance, sherry vinegar for soups and sauces, raspberry vinegar for deglazing, pear vinegar on fruit salad, or mixed with sliced strawberries and bananas. Balsamic vinegar, a very dark, sharp-flavored vinegar, made since the tenth century and aged as wines are, is used for sauces, marinades, deglazes, and is wonderful with a sauté of veal. Marigold vinegar, a fine white-wine vinegar in which a marigold has been steeped, is suggested for fruit salad and fish.

Walnut oil is used for flavor; hazelnut oil is wonderful brushed onto a cake pan in which layer cakes are baked, and almond oil brushed on fish before broiling gives it a flavor that is unusual yet delicious.

Cold pressed fine virgin olive oil is very green. The flavor is almost peppery and definitely different—rich and fullbodied.

Dinah marinates edible flowers, such as nasturtiums and marigolds, in either sterile vinegar or very fine olive oil. These make wonderful little gifts, particularly if they're packaged in attractive, small bottles. And hostesses love to receive them.

Harvey Kirck's Barbecue Sauce

Harvey is on a diet this year and his specialties seem to range from cottage cheese with green onions to boiled eggs. However, he kindly agreed to show us some of his favorite recipes for preparing on the boat. This sauce is delicious with hamburgers, steak, ribs and chicken. (Makes 2 cups of sauce)

Ingredients

1	cup ketchup	2	teaspoons dried mustard
1	cup vinegar	2	teaspoons Worcestershire sauce
½	cup water		
½	cup chopped onion	1	teaspoon Tobasco sauce
2	tablespoons sugar	½	teaspoon black pepper

Method

Combine all ingredients in a saucepan and heat for 5 minutes.

Barbecue Sauce

(Makes 3 cups)

Ingredients

2	cups soy sauce	4	teaspoons dry mustard
4	tablespoons basil	4	cloves garlic, pulverized
4	tablespoons rosemary	4	teaspoons salt
4	tablespoons sugar		Juice of 4 lemons

Method

Place the above ingredients in a small pan and slowly bring to the simmering point. Simmer for 2–3 minutes and set aside to cool. Add the lemon juice. Pour over the meat and let stand one hour or so before barbecuing. Then baste frequently while cooking.

Keep sauce sealed in sterilized jars.

Chinese 5-Spice Powder

Usually, if you are planning to prepare Chinese food, a trip to an Oriental market is called for. If so, 5-Spice powder is easily available. If you have difficulty, here is a substitute. It keeps for a year.

Ingredients

2	tablespoons cracked black peppercorns	12	whole star anise
12	sticks whole cinnamon bark (about 2–3 inches each)	30	whole cloves
		2	tablespoons fennel seeds

Method

Grind all of the ingredients, using a pestle and mortar, food processor, blender or hand grinder.

Homemade Horseradish

Choose a good, firm horseradish root, or piece of root, and make your own horseradish. This will keep in the refrigerator for about 6 weeks, or in the freezer for 6 months. It tastes sharp and delicious. One-quarter pound horseradish root will give you 1 cup of grated horseradish.

Ingredients

¼	pound horseradish root	½	teaspoon salt
3	tablespoons vinegar	½	teaspoon sugar

Method

Slice the horseradish in half and soak in cold water. It's best to do this the night before. Peel and cut into cubes.

Food Processor Method
Using the grating disc, process the horseradish quickly, add the balance of the ingredients, blend together and store in the refrigerator in a jar.

Blender Method
Add cold water to cover the blade, add diced horseradish and process. If you do not add enough water the root will be pulverized before it is processed. Drain the water carefully through a sieve. Combine the sieved horseradish with the balance of the ingredients and store in a clean jar in the refrigerator.

Cranberry Ketchup

From Cranberrie Cottage, Nova Scotia, comes this recipe for cranberry ketchup. Beatrice Buszek writes movingly about her berry fields and the memories they hold for herself and her family. (Makes 6 pints)

Ingredients

1	pound (500 g) onions	1	tablespoon ground cloves
4	pounds (2 kg) cranberries	1	tablespoon cinnamon
2	cups water	1	tablespoon allspice
2	cups vinegar	1	teaspoon salt
4	cups sugar		Pinch of pepper

Method

Peel onions and chop finely, add berries and water and cook. Rub through a sieve. Add remaining ingredients and boil until thick, stirring occasionally. Pour into hot jars and seal. Serve as a relish.

Mint Sauce
(Makes ½ cup)

Ingredients

1	large handful fresh mint leaves	3	tablespoons white wine vinegar
	Sugar		Pinch of salt
2	tablespoons boiling water		
1	tablespoon fine sugar		

Method

Chop the mint finely or pound in a mortar until smooth with a little sugar. Turn into a bowl and add boiling water. This will set the color. Stir in the fine sugar and vinegar and season with salt. Taste and add more sugar if necessary. The sauce should be bright green and thick in consistency. Pour into a jar and refrigerate.

Mint sauce is traditionally served with lamb.

Lemon Curd

Mention lemon curd to an Englishman or Scotsman and you can see his mouth water. It's a simple spread for muffins or biscuits that has the sweetness of jam and the tartness of lemons. (Makes 4–5 1-cup jars)

Ingredients

6	eggs, well beaten	½	cup lemon juice + zest
2	cups sugar	¼	cup butter

Method

Combine all the ingredients except butter in the top of a double boiler. Cook until thick, then add the butter. Stir to blend together. Pour into sterilized jars and seal.

Use this as filling for pies or cakes or as a spread.

Lemon Marmalade

Make as few as 2 or as many as 6 jars of marmalade at a time with this recipe. I have given the amounts for 6 1-cup jars but you can cut this down to accommodate the number of lemons that you have.

Ingredients

6	washed but unpeeled lemons, sliced very thinly and cut crosswise into small pieces	Water
		Sugar

Method

Measure the fruit and add three times as much water to a heavy saucepan. Add the fruit and boil together for 20 minutes or until the fruit and peel are tender. Measure and add water to replace the liquid that has boiled away. Allow ¾ cup sugar for each cup of fruit juice. Cook for 1 hour and then test. Remove pot from the heat, place a bit of marmalade on a cold plate that has been stored in the freezer. Chill it immediately for 1 minute in the refrigerator. Your marmalade is ready when the chilled marmalade on the plate wrinkles if pushed with a finger. Pour into sterilized jelly jars and seal.

Banana Ginger Chutney

(Makes 5½ pints or 2.5 L)

Ingredients

⅔	cup molasses	12	ripe bananas (approximately 3 pounds or 1.4 kg)
1	cup water		
2	cups cider vinegar	2	pounds (900 g) Bermuda onions, chopped coarsely
½	teaspoon ground ginger		
1	teaspoon allspice	2	cups pitted dates, chopped
1	teaspoon salt		

Method

Preheat oven to 350°F. In a non-aluminum flat pan combine molasses, water and vinegar. Add ginger, allspice and salt. Peel and cut bananas into small pieces, add to liquids with the onions and dates. Bake for about 1 hour. Pour into sterilized jars and seal. Let rest for 2 months.

Horseradish Sauce

(Makes 1 cup)

Ingredients

2	heaped tablespoons freshly grated horseradish	4	teaspoons white wine vinegar
½	teaspoon dry mustard	¼	pint heavy cream
	Pinch of sugar		Salt and pepper to taste

Method

Mix together the horseradish, mustard, sugar and vinegar and blend well. Whip the cream lightly and mix carefully with the other ingredients. Season with salt and pepper. Pour into a jar and refrigerate.

Pear, Apple, Nut Chutney
(Makes 3 quarts or 2.5 L approximately)

Ingredients

5	cups cider vinegar		2	teaspoons cinnamon
1	cup candied ginger		1	teaspoon salt
2	large onions		1	teaspoon cayenne
4	oranges		1	6-ounce (170 g) package
5	pounds (2.5 kg) firm pears			dehydrated apples, diced
2	pounds (900 g) light brown			Water
	sugar		2	cups walnuts, toasted and
2	15-ounce (425 g) boxes raisins			chopped
2	teaspoons cloves			

Method

Pour vinegar into large kettle. Chop ginger, onions and oranges finely. Add to vinegar. Core and slice the pears but do not peel, add to vinegar with remaining dry ingredients. Add water: the amount of water needed depends on the dryness of the pears—it may take as little as 2–4 cups or as much as 8–10 cups of water. Stir. Simmer until thick, about $1\frac{1}{2}$–$2\frac{1}{2}$ hours. Just before putting into jars, add walnuts. Seal.

To Sterilize Jars

Oven Method
Set clean jars on rack in oven. Heat to 250°F for at least 10 minutes. Remove from oven when needed, allowing to cool slightly.

Boiling Water Method
Cover the washed jars with hot water inside a large kettle or invert them in 1–2 inches of water. Bring to the boil and continue to boil for 15 minutes. Leave in hot water until needed.

RECIPE CREDITS

Many celebrity guests and chefs were generous with their time and in sharing techniques and recipes that are included in this book. To all I am grateful.

Werner Bassin, Executive Chef
Fenton's Restaurant
Toronto

Janet Berton
Canadian Food Guide
McClelland & Stewart Publishers
Toronto

Beef Information Centre
Toronto

John Clancy
324 West 19th Street
New York

Gay Cook
76 Lakeshore
Morrisburg, Ontario

Roger Dufau, Executive Chef
Maison Basque Restaurant
Toronto

Dufflet
Dufflet's Pastries
Toronto

Harvey Kirck
CTV News
Toronto

Niels Kjeldson, Executive Chef
Four Seasons Hotel—Yorkville
Toronto

Meta and Jeanette McCall
McCall's School of Cake Decoration Ltd.
Islington, Ontario

Françoise Monnet, Chef
Les Parisiennes Restaurant
Toronto

Dacia Moss, Manager
Epicure Shop
Holt Renfrew & Company
Toronto

Margo Oliver
Toronto Star
Toronto

Sandra O'Neill
O'Neill's Dinner Theatre
Willowdale, Ontario

Jane Rodmell
"Epicure"
Toronto Life Magazine
Toronto

Mary Risley
Tante Marie's Cooking School
San Francisco, California

Alex Schur
Steward—CP Air
Vancouver International Airport

Herbert Sonszogni, Executive Chef
Babsi's Restaurant
Mississauga, Ontario

Bonnie Stern
Bonnie Stern's School of Cooking
Toronto

Michael Vaughan
Michael's Mussels
Toronto

Lucy Waverman
204 Glenayr Road
Toronto

Index

Please note that an *M* after an entry in this index denotes that microwave instructions are provided.

Almond cookies, rolled, 120
Appetizers, 9-16
Apple
  muffins, 111
  strudel, 129
  tart maison Basque, 130
  with cinnamon, 130
Applesauce
  apple flan, 129
  bran muffins, 111
Apricot
  upside down cake, 116, *M*
  yogurt dessert, 126
Armagnac prune soufflé, 131
Artichokes Roman style, 90
Aspic, quick, 14

Bagels, 106
Banana ginger chutney, 149
Barbecue sauce, 146
  Harvey Kirck's, 145
Beef, 26-38
  crusty—and vegetable pie, 37
  steak and kidney pie, 31
  and vegetable stew, 30
Beer soup, 19
Beet and cabbage borscht, 18
Beets in nippy cream sauce, 89
Biscuits, baking powder, 106
Bran muffins, best, 112
Breads, 103-109
Butter sauce, 143, *M*

Cakes, 115-117
Canneloni stuffed with chicken, 54, *M*
Carrot
  -honey bran muffins, 113
  -pineapple muffins, 112
Casserole
  carefree, 36, *M*
  eggplant, 84, *M*
  pork and fruit, 40
  pork and lemon, 39
Cheese
  apple, snappy, 10
  finger snaps, 10
  soufflé for two, 77, *M*
  wafers, 11

Cheesecake
  Bonnie Stern's chocolate, 138
  Bonnie Stern's lemon, 137
Cherry soufflé pudding, 133
Chicken
  canneloni stuffed with, 54, *M*
  in a clay baker, 52, *M*
  in crystal fold, 50
  curried with shrimp, 48
  curry O'Neill, 49, *M*
  pot pie, 53
  turkey or — strata, 55
Chili, vegetarian, 87
Chinese
  5-spice powder, 146
  pork and pineapple, 42
  ribs, 42
Chocolate
  applesauce cake, 139
  cake, 117, *M*
  cheesecake, Bonnie Stern's, 138
  chip meringue cake, 138-139
  soufflé, 140
Chutney
  banana ginger, 149
  pear, apple, nut, 150
Clarified butter, 35
Cookies, 119-121
Cornish hen, roasted, (Kamama), 58
Cracked wheat salad, 97
Cranberry ketchup, 147
Cream cheese
  hearts with fruit, 142
  tartlet shells, 127
Crêpes soufflé roxelane, 132
Croissants, 108-109
Cross rib roast, 26
Croutons, diced, 24
Cuts of beef, 26

Danish pastry, 118-119
Desserts, 122-143
Dumplings, 23

Eggplant casserole, 84, *M*
Eggs
  and fried rice, 94
  hunter's, 76

Escargots bourguignon, 16

Fettucine all' Alfredo, 80
Fig pudding, 137
Fish, 62-73
    baked—with mussels and broccoli,
        70, *M*
    creole—with rice, 68, *M*
    in parchment, 63
    stock, mock, 67
Fisherman's chowder in crust, 64
Floating islands, 142
French toast, bridge club foamy, 76
Fruit mousse with hazelnuts, 125

Garlic bread, Gruyère, 107
Gnocchi di patate, 86, *M*
Goulash soup with dumplings, 22
Gratin
    dauphinois à la crème, 89, *M*
    of greens, 90, *M*
Ground beef facts, 31
Grouper, marinated, 15
Gruyère garlic bread, 107

Ham and Cheddar strata, 78
Hazelnut cookies, twice-baked, 119
Heart soup, Janet's, 38
Holiday refrigerator cookies, 121
Honey butter, 113
Horseradish
    homemade, 146
    sauce, 149

Kasha and vegetable pie, 85, *M*

Lamb m'shwi, 45
    noisettes of, with basil cream
        sauce, 46
Leek and potato soup, creamy, 24
Lemon
    cheesecake, Bonnie Stern's, 137
    curd, 148
    flan, 134-135
    jelly, Pierre's favorite, 123
    marmalade, 148
    and strawberry sherbet, 123
Lime soufflé, cold, 124

Mackerel, baked, 65, *M*
Marinade
    #1, 29
    #2, 30

Meat
    glaze, 28
    and rice salad, hot, 33
Meatballs, little hot, 34
Melba sauce, 133
Melon wedges with Parma ham, 11
Mint sauce, 148
Moroccan
    carrot salad, 99
    cucumber salad, 99
Muffins, 111-114
Mussels in black bean sauce, 69
Mushroom(s)
    celery and Swiss cheese salad, 97
    spinach and pepper salad, 98
Mustard sauce, 15

Noisettes of lamb with basil cream
    sauce, 46

Oils and vinegars, fancy, 145
Omelette soufflé, 134-135

Parsley vinaigrette, 98
Pâté
    en croûte, John Clancy's, 12
    late day, 14
Pea soup, fresh, 19
Pear
    apple nut chutney, 150
    -cranberry pudding, steamed,
        135, *M*
Penne alla vodka, 81
Pepper
    mayonnaise, 11
    steak, 35
Pork, 39-44
    chops, breaded, 43, *M*
    and fruit casserole, 40
    and lemon casserole, 39
    rolls with mushroom and ham
        filling, 40, *M*
    and vegetable salad, 44
Pot roast with crab apples, 27
Potato salad, hot, 101
Poulet basquaise, 51
Poultry, 47-61
Pudding
    cherry soufflé, 133
    fig, 136
    steamed pear-cranberry, 135, *M*
Pumpkin soup, Charlie Brown's, 21

Rabbit with honey and tomato
    sauce, 58
Rhubarb custard, 125
Rice
  cooking tips for, 92, *M*
  egg and fried—, 94
  Milanese-style, 94
  pilaf, 93
Roast
  cross rib, 26
  —duck with Normandy sauce, 60
  pot—with crab apples, 27

Sabayon sauce with Marsala, 143
Salads, 97-102
Salmon in puff pastry with sorrel
    sauce, 66
Sauce
  barbecue, 145, 146
  butter, 143, *M*
  horseradish, 149
  melba, 133
  mint, 148
  mustard, 15
  Normandy, 61
  sorrel, 66-67
  sabayon with Marsala, 143
  tomato, 59
Short ribs, spiced, 28
Shrimp
  hot and spicy—soup, 20
  with lemon and ginger, 71
  sauté of—with wild rice, mush-
    rooms and tomato, 72
Sole with apple, 67
Soufflé
  Armagnac prune, 131
  cheese, 77, *M*
  chocolate, 140
  cold lime, 124
  omelette, 134-135

Soups, 17-24
Spaghetti
  alla puttanesca, 73
  fresh tomato, garlic and basil, 83
  quick—with creamy tomato
    sauce, 82
  springtime, 82
Spinach
  salad with hot bacon dressing, 100
  salad with hot chicken livers, 100
Stew, beef and vegetable, 30
Sweetbread salad, hot, 102

Tiramisu', 141
Tofu
  grilled—sandwich, 80
  lasagna, 79, *M*
Turkey
  terrine, 56
  or chicken strata, 55

Veal birds jardinière, 44
Vegetable
  flan, 95, *M*
Vegetables, 88-95
Vegetarian chili, 87

Whole-grain buttermilk bread, 104
Whole-wheat
  corn muffins, 114, *M*
  pumpkin muffins, 114
Winter
  fruit salad, 126-127
  salad, 101

Yogurt
  barley and chicken soup, 23
  coffee cake, 115, *M*